WORK HORSE

**From an Amish Farm
to the NFL Gridiron**

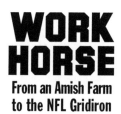

WORK HORSE
From an Amish Farm
to the NFL Gridiron

by
ZACH OLSTAD
with Melody Olstad

"...To make it to the NFL from a Division II school is a tribute to Zach's tremendous work ethic and perseverance. We can all be inspired by the path Zach Olstad took to get to Buffalo."

Sean McDermott
Head Coach, Buffalo Bills

"...As the Head Coach of a Division II Football program you seek to sign recruits that dream of playing in the NFL! Zach Olstad worked every day to just have a chance! His passion to be the very best, lead 120 teammates along the way! Zach Olstad committed his entire soul to our program and the result was his "NFL Dream" came true!"

Tom Sawyer
Head Coach, Winona State University

"...As a college football player, Zach epitomized the definition of hard work, commitment and faith. His football journey took him from a Division II walk-on to a 4-year starter, worked through serious injuries to come back to play at Winona State, and make it to the NFL. Having had the chance to know Zach and his family over the last 10 years, it's easy to see that Zach is a true Warrior whose ability to outwork his competitors to achieve his dreams is inspiring."

Cameron Keller
Offensive Coordinator, Winona State University

"...Having been given the privilege to explore Zach's book, it's a page-turner; full of perspiration and inspiration, interwoven with life-lessons, quotable wisdom... and a little football, too. *Work Horse* will take you from an Amish Farm to the NFL Gridiron and leave you believing in whatever field you find."

Barton Green
Author

To my Dad, Mom, Brother and Sister:

*You have always inspired me to be the
hardest worker I can be,
and to reach for my greatest potential.*

I owe you everything.

Contents

Preface. 11

1 Yard Lessons 13
  #OlstadsInsteads

2 Farm-Bred Fundamentals 23
  #OlstadsInsteads

3 Sharpening Tools. 33
  #OlstadsInsteads

4 Rhythm of The Grind 45
  #OlstadsInsteads

5 Warrior Code 61
  #OlstadsInsteads

6 Porch Pacin'. 79
  #OlstadsInsteads

7 The Call. 89
  #OlstadsInsteads

8 One More. 97
  #OlstadsInsteads

9 Organized Team Activities 111
  #OlstadsInsteads

10 Driven 119
    #OlstadsInsteads

11 Stumble Forward 127
    #OlstadsInsteads

    Epilogue 141

    Acknowledgements 143

Preface

I thought that getting a contract in the NFL would be the hardest thing that I could ever do in life, but then I started writing this book. I quickly learned that our biggest challenges and greatest endeavors are never in the past, but in the present and future. I gained a new understanding and perspective on my career but more importantly, my life. Over the years, I overcame impossible odds in order to pursue my dream. I hope that sharing my story encourages you to realize that if I can do it, you can do it too.

I grew up in a small Minnesota farming town, surrounded by corn fields, green pastures outlined by fence posts and Amish neighbors in every direction. I grew up running from our creek to the kitchen at the sound of my Mom swinging a lunch bell, feeding calves before dawn, and then riding with my Dad to school. My roots run deep in Amish country, but even as a kid I was driven by dreams beyond my daily life. I grew up loving the game of football and if my life was a movie, it would be an 80s-Sports film starring a guy in a sleeveless sweatshirt, flipping tires as a workout before jumping on the tractor. I have lived in wonder of what is humanly possible and surprised myself at every turn. Along the way I risked everything, transcending self-doubt, and fear, in order to pursue something unimaginable.

I would not trade that small town, or my childhood on the farm for anything; that time and place was the beginning of my journey. There I learned how to hang on, how to take a hit, and master the art of sticking with it. Back then was when I first imagined my improbable path to Buffalo.

1

Yard Lessons

Some people outgrow their childhood dreams, and some are too scared to pursue them.

The last time that I left Nashville for a trip home to Harmony, MN I walked into my childhood bedroom and saw that my Mom had framed a small drawing that I had once made of a lopsided football with the letters NFL written on it. The white construction paper had yellowed, but the image was clear. Hanging on the wall next to this masterpiece was a photo of my college football team, and next to that, a framed Buffalo Bills game jersey, number 36. Mom had transformed my old room into a mini museum, complete with a closet full of all my old jerseys and cleats, each with a story to tell.

Looking at that 20-year-old drawing and the many strides I've made since then, I realized that my childhood dream had been unthinkable, unbelievable, and well worth the fight.

***

My parents often joked about how quickly I went from crawling to running. This was mainly due to my older brother and sister. There is no mercy for the youngest child. In fact, the greatest joy for my devious siblings was to chase after me with a handful of worms.

I was four years old, enjoying a peaceful afternoon in my sandbox, when the first worm was put down my pants. Years of worm-induced trauma followed, but I eventually found my feet and became the fastest little kid on my block.

In those early years, we lived on a dead-end street in a neighborhood called Corn Cob Acres in Preston, MN. We were surrounded by other families with kids around our same age. A total of fifteen or so lived on our street, and yes, I was the runt. Not only was I the youngest, but I was an undersized child, and a late bloomer. I didn't hit my growth spurt until I was sixteen and my prayers were finally heard.

Being the youngest and the smallest on the block, I had no choice but to keep up or get left behind. The one advantage was that I learned from watching the older kids. This proved to be true when I was moved up to play Babe Ruth baseball on my older brother's team.

Levi has always been my role model. When I first joined his team's roster, I was easily a foot shorter, and at least four years younger than the rest of the team. And of course, I was bumped to the bottom of the batting order.

When it was finally my turn at the plate, my small hands barely choked the bat. Ahead, towering over me on the mound, was the pitcher, smiling down at me through the grizzle of his already fully-grown beard.

But being small sometimes has its advantages

and the pitcher could not find my strike zone. I walked to first. Then made my way to third base. From there, I was in position to score.

The pitcher suddenly threw a wild pitch. With the dugout screaming "GO" and the third base coach giving me the green light, I took off.

As I slid into home base, everything turned into slow motion. I saw the umpire signal "Sa-a-aafe!" But as I looked down to my knee, I saw blood seeping through my baseball pants and the cheers turned to gasps.

Laying there at home base, I recognized my brother's voice from the dugout, "Get up!" Though I was in pain, I managed to limp over to him. Rolling up my pants we watched a gush of blood spew from my knee thanks to a slash from the pitcher's cleat.

Immediately, we all piled in the car for the doctor's office. It was my first, but far from my last, sports-related injury.

When I say "we" that always included Mom. She was our chief cook and chauffeur; the one who perpetually fed and ferried us to and from school, church, tryouts, practice and—no matter how near or far—every game. Mom was always there, at my side from the dugout to the doctor's office. Her constant worries and unconditional love has been our source and shield against everything from potential dehydration to hurling foul balls.

Dad was at most of our events as well, but in the summer, he would be busy farming, doing field work, or painting houses to make extra money. When he got home that night and heard the news of my first injury, he came to the room that I shared with my older brother and asked if I was alright. I showed him my fresh stitches and he smiled, "you'll be okay, that's a long way from your heart."

If we ever got hurt while playing in the yard or on the field, he would always tell us to walk it off and know the difference between pain and an injury. Knowing the difference was ingrained in me at a young age. It was the decision to tap out or test your limits and see how far you can push yourself. I am lucky to have been given two supportive, loving parents who, despite the constant mayhem, always balanced everything out.

***

When my folks first married, Dad went to college during the day and worked at a Lefse Factory in the evenings, where he made $2.50 per hour making Norwegian Flatbread. Mom worked at a nursing home, and their schedules were so hectic they hardly saw each other. Once he graduated college, Dad snagged a job as a teacher and basketball coach in the neighboring town of Preston. And from then on, the two started saving up for their dream home in the country.

In the evenings, Dad would do field work for a local farmer and each night one of us kids got to ride along. Often Mom would come out to the field and bring us dinner.

My siblings and I would fight over who would get to join Dad in the tractor. But no matter which of us won, we would usually fall asleep on the little seat next to him and wake up in pain from our heads banging against the tractor window. I am still not sure if I got my first concussion on those bumpy tractor rides, or on the football field.

Finally, after years of saving and tirelessly working, my parents found their dream home. In October of 1999, they closed on a 64-acre farm with a small creek running through the property. Mom found the farm in a local newspaper article. It had been previously owned by an Amish family.

Changing Yards

I wasn't a very tough six-year-old, leaving my childhood home and all those backyard games. But, as soon as I realized we had 64 acres to explore, this little Olstad was a happy farmer.

Driving down the back roads, you approach an Amish schoolhouse, which is still in use to this day. This old schoolhouse sits at the top of our driveway. Our new driveway was a long gravel road that curved down through a wooded hillside and an open pasture, leading to a massive old barn and an old, dilapidated Amish house. Surrounding the two structures was a sweeping pasture divided by a slow meandering creek, which after a storm would turn into a small river. We were home. And it wasn't long before my family started transforming the 64 acres into our own country slice of heaven.

For the first seven months we lived in the old Amish house, while building our forever home. Most days that first summer, we were climbing the hill up to the construction site at the break of dawn. When we had a break from building, us kids would run down to the creek to swim, fish, and catch all sorts of bugs. We were ecstatic, living the dream.

***

Our childhood neighbors in Preston, MN were

backyard athletes and our best friends, but once we moved to the farm in Harmony, our strange new neighbors opened up a whole land of lessons.

By their nature, the Amish coexist. Once we moved to the country, they became our fast friends. In fact, Dad immediately hired them to help us build the new house. The 'people of the old way' are excellent carpenters. It didn't take long before we felt at home and learned the ancient, local art of trading favors. And when it came to their rare brand of bartering, none was more interesting than getting a phone call, in the middle of the night.

When I was growing up the locals didn't use phones unless there was an emergency. So, we knew when our landline rang in the middle of the night, it was most likely a neighbor in need. The Community only traveled by horse and buggy, so if they called to ask for a ride from their "English" neighbors, we knew it was important. If, for instance, a local mother-to-be could not give birth at home, my parents would get a call asking for a ride to the nearest midwife. Or, more often than not, my folks would pick up the midwife and ferry her to her client. If a non-emergency ride was needed, we would hear our dogs barking at the rickety sound of horse and buggy coming down our long hill to schedule the trip.

The Amish lifestyle had an inviting, simple charm. By simply living around them, my family developed a deep regard for the community. With four seasons in Minnesota and a brutal winter, you develop a quick respect for the Amish as they heat their home with a wood burning stove and wrap themselves up with blankets as they travel the harsh roads in open-air buggies.

The simple lifestyle left such an impact on us, that my parents did not get internet until I was well into college. And being that their first connection was dial-up, you could describe the service as "Basic Amish Wi-Fi." My folks have yet to experience cable in their home.

In my new yard, I learned early on what it was like to live without. During the construction of the new house, we camped out in the old one—or better put, we survived there.

The farm had no electricity. Nights were dark and spooky. I had my own room in the Amish house, but was I ever sleeping in it? Did I mention I was 6? I don't recall a time that I slept a full night in that room alone. I would start the evenings in my bed but quickly get spooked and sneak into my brother's room. Some nights he would kick me out and I would sleep on an old rummaged pool table in his room where at least I wasn't alone. The fun was over for me during the nighttime.

The old house was tucked away down the long curving driveway and was the very last building the driveway leads to. In front of the house was a towering, creaky windmill that sounded like something out of a scary movie. The house was surrounded by a variety of towering trees including oak, pine, and walnut. Connected to the Amish house was an old summer room where the Amish would keep their perishables cool, an outhouse (the only bathroom that the Amish had used) still half full from the previous tenants, and a small outbuilding that we called the wood shed.

It was all connected by one brick sidewalk. The sidewalk went around the house and up the grass towards the driveway. Right next to the sidewalk standing over the house was a big walnut tree, the branches of which reached out to my room's window and roof. It was like taking a step back into the year 1910, a world before our time full of lush woods and gardens but no electricity or running water. Although the nighttime was one of my greatest fears as a six-year-old, I worked up the courage to sleep in my own room after a few months. It wasn't long before I heard what I thought was a ghost or someone trying to break into my room. Later that night after losing it and running into my parent's room, we discovered that the big tree outside of my window was a gateway for a raccoon family that had come to live above my room in the roof. I never slept in that room again.

Thankfully, one of our relatives was an electrician. We wired a couple lights so we weren't totally out of luck when the sun went down, but it was minimal and I was still scared. Being in a dark old house in the middle of the night and having to use the bathroom was one of the worst feelings for 6-year-old me.

No plumbing meant more than just no toilet, it created a whole world of complications for my younger self. There was an outhouse that hadn't been emptied by the previous tenant before we moved in. Needless to say, it was terrifying to use. There were three holes cut out on the seat with two large rings for adults and one small ring for children to use. I was always afraid that I would fall in or that something would come up to bite me. Often, I would be in pain holding my bladder in the dead of the night, too scared to venture outside my room but in serious need of the bathroom.

During the daytime, I would just pee outside or off the porch. I did that so often that there was a dead spot in the grass.

It got worse as fall became winter. Minnesota is cold to begin with. No furnace made the house extremely cold in the wintertime. Waking up was a constant battle of racing to breakfast to sit by the one little space heater we had. There wasn't room for everyone by the heater so there was usually someone eating breakfast in a winter jacket with blankets. I will say this didn't last forever. Luckily, we weren't in the Amish house through the harshest winter months, but there were definitely days where I was ready to be living my normal life again.

***

Although this lifestyle was challenging as a young kid, I wouldn't be where I am today without it. The fears that I had to overcome, the work ethic that I began to be molded by, and the mindset that with the right attitude and will to succeed you can get through anything, paved the way for my journey as life went on. But the farming and blue-collar lifestyle didn't just go away once we finally moved into our completed home at the top of the hill and moved out of the Amish house. In fact, the work was just getting started.

***

#OlstadsInsteads

There's an excuse for everything if you want to use it. Instead, create your own slice of heaven with the hand you were dealt.

From our new front yard amongst an old culture, I had to learn the hard lessons to find my own field of dreams.

2

Farm-Bred Fundamentals

You cannot escape the fundamentals. The principles that form the foundations of your experience are all around you. What you are first taught at a kid's camp or in math class, creates the foundation for what you will learn next. And these experiences form the foundation of who you eventually become, what you believe, and what you are willing to do to reach your dreams.

The fundamentals are different for everyone. But learning from them, and building upon those mental and physical repetitions, will last a lifetime. For me, the fundamental principles of my life were forged on the back roads of rural Minnesota.

If you blink while driving through the Southeastern part of the state, you might miss the scattered, small-town city limit signs boasting a few hundred souls. A tourist might even find the landscape boring. But for those who grew up farming and living the small-town life, this little corner of the world is our everything.

Almost everyone I know in our area has family in farming. My relatives lived on a farm thirty minutes down the road from ours, and when we weren't working on our chores at home, we were usually there helping with their operation. Their farm was a much larger operation, with crops and cattle. If there was nothing else to do, Dad assured us that we would never be done fixing fences.

Callused Hands

We grew up spending our summers working from sunup to sundown doing everything from stacking bales in the humid heat, to hilling potatoes in the garden. There was always machinery to maintain, crops to harvest and a fence to mend. But of these many summer farm chores, 'baling' was always my favorite.

My brother and I would climb up into the hay wagon and stack while Dad drove the tractor/baler. The job was simple: as a square bale of hay would spit out of the baler, we would quickly handle those heavy bundles and stack each one as fast as we could, hoping we didn't get suckered by an ill-timed flying block. The most we ever stacked in one day was close to 2,000 bales, which was a "good day's work."

Having grown up on the busy end of a bale wagon, Dad enjoyed this game of dodge the bale, especially when we were old enough to keep our balance on the wagon. Often, just for fun, Dad would aim a bale at us, laughing at our comical attempts to dodge the incoming. Farming is hard work, especially in the extremes of Midwestern weather, but it taught me that working hard is extremely rewarding and a lot of fun. The camaraderie that my Dad and Mom created within our family by making hard work fun set the standard for my future work ethic. I carried these lessons from the farm into my mentality in sports and in life.

Some chores on the farm built strength, while others built character. I was six years old when I learned how to drive a car and then a tractor. My parents always kept a beat-up car that we would use to run errands and at the time they owned a Caprice Classic. We had just harvested our soybean field outside of Harmony when Dad tossed me the keys. Seeing that the field was empty, I was given the green light to crank up the old Caprice Classic and take her for a spin.

I could barely see over the wheel. But I slowly worked that boat-sized vehicle and learned the basics. There was plenty of room for error so my Dad and Mom would let us take it out and learn first-hand how to drive. When in doubt, I would hit the brakes and hope for the best. But the old car wasn't just for driving lessons.

Like our Amish neighbors, we raised Holstein calves, and were looking to add to our stock. But back then we didn't have a convenient way to haul calves. So, we turned our old car into a makeshift cattle trailer.

Once Dad and the Amish shook hands on the price, Levi and I loaded up a couple of week-old calves into the back seat of the Caprice. My brother and I would wrap the calves in a blanket and bear hug them throughout the short ride home in case they tried to kick. It wasn't the safest way to haul calves but as kids we were simply excited to have a new calf to bring home. The worst that would happen is that the calf would kick, try to head butt you, or get nervous and poop in the backseat.

Clearly, we had very little to worry about.

Between the ages of seven and twelve, I would go with the family to Decorah, Iowa and buy 100–200 baby chickens. These golden, fluffy chicks were the most adorable little creatures. But over the weeks their cuteness faded fast. First, they lost their golden feathers. Then, as they grew, so did the smell. And once the birds were big enough, my family would prepare the kitchen in the house, set up the different butcher stations outside, and get ready for butchering weekend. This was a weekend that my siblings and I grew to dread. My Dad would use an old stump as his butchering block to chop the heads off. Once he chopped the head off he would hand the bird to one of us to let the blood drain. We would hold the feet with the feathers pinned and if the bird wiggled out of your grip, they could still run great distances after their heads have been chopped off. We would then dip the bird in a pot of boiling hot water and pluck the feathers off. This process lasted all day as we slowly butchered all of the chickens, prepped them, and stocked the deep freezer. My parents enjoyed the farm to table experience by raising animals and growing vegetables. My Dad had butchered chickens with his family when he was growing up, so he figured we could do the same. However, it was much less common to do this in 2004 versus 1984, so it wasn't something I would tell my friends at school.

Every morning before school the entire family would be up before the sun, caring for our vast acreage of sprouting fields as well as our menagerie of cows, chickens, and horses.

Our Holstein veal calves would be bellowing with anticipation every morning while we carried hot pails of milk replacer down to them. We would pour each a helping into a bucket or bottle. At least a few calves would not cooperate, so we would have to dump the milk in a pail, stick our hand in the pail, and then let them suck on our fingers, so they would think it was a teat. Sometimes the calf would all but rip your fingers off with their sharp, newborn teeth. When hungry, little calves are strong. In fact, after a few weeks of helping the calves drink out of a bucket, my little hand was a freak show display of cuts, bruises, and teeth marks.

Caring for the Holstein calves and our eventual herd of Angus cattle ingrained a sense of responsibility and accountability into my daily routine. So many factors make a good calving season. From feeding and vaccinating the herd along with securing a good bull to impregnate all of the cows, to checking the population for pregnancy. Every step must be done properly to ensure the safety of both farmer and the herd.

The most fulfilling step with the Angus herd is calving season, when the cows begin to have their calves. Our herd calved in the Minnesota winter. Calving during the winter months is a constant battle of fighting the cold, making sure your expecting cows are in a warm-bedded pen when their due date is approaching, and always making sure to check on the entire herd throughout the day in case of a cow having a calf early. Keeping an eye on the cows is important because if they have difficulties calving, they need immediate attention and possibly need us to "pull" the calf. When we had to pull a calf, we would walk the birthing cow into a pen and corner it off so that it couldn't escape. After securing the cow, we would then tie twine around the calf's hooves. Once the hooves were tied my Dad would maneuver the calf into proper birthing position and my brother and I would slowly and steadily pull the calf out. This is no easy task. If a cow is having trouble giving birth, you can quickly lose the calf and potentially the mother. In most cases the calf and the cow live, but if you're not present when the cow is trying to give birth, you can easily lose the calf. Pulling and pulling while the twine is ripping at your hands isn't for the faint of heart. Farming teaches you gratitude as you watch the circle of life unfold and you always sacrifice what you can to help your farm. The experiences that I had on the farm, the good and the bad, quickly found their way into my attitude and work ethic. I have carried all of these life lessons with me and they have become the key to my success as an athlete, family member, and friend.

Farm Training

I didn't start officially training until I was in the fifth grade, when my brother started dragging me into the weight room.

Before then, I was doing simple, makeshift workouts using what was available around the farm. From flipping old tractor tires, to chopping at old tires with a maul, I always found a way to workout. When I got sick of flipping and hitting things, Dad and Levi made me a cinder block pull. Wrapping an old horse rope around me, I attached the other end to a dragging tire with a cinder block passenger. I'd sprint up and down our yard with that contraption until I could barely breathe or walk. Was it fancy? Not at all, but it got the job done.

Another great workout on the farm was hill sprints. Steep hills on our farm were carved with a path straight up and down. That's where I spent most of my afternoons. Up and down that hill I went with my dogs until I was too tired to go anymore. That torture taught my body great control and gave my legs a workout like no other.

Hill sprints, flipping tires, mauling tires, and pulling the old cinder block, combined with push-ups and sit-ups, was the bulk of my fifth-grade regimen. It was neither fancy nor was it the most proven technique, but I worked with what I had. And did it every day, without fail.

In those early years, I trained just to keep up with my parents and older siblings for our standard Sunday games. The sprawling farm definitely had the room for it. Up by the house, we would play football in a part of the yard that resembled a football field. And down by the creek, we built a backstop and mowed a baseball diamond into the pasture.

My folks always emphasized that having fun and giving it your all applied to both work and play. And for that reason, I always wanted to be on Dad's team, because he would do everything in his power to win. I remember watching him dive to catch a football and bust a rib, as he rolled down the hill. He walked it off just like he had taught us to. And never once did he visit a doctor.

So, no matter how rowdy those family farm games got, I always dived in and never backed down. However, if things got too out of hand, Mom would swoop in at just the right time, and tell us that dinner was ready.

***

Once fifth grade came along, I rode to school with my brother and Dad. By then Levi was in high school and I was in middle school, making me even more determined to keep up with him, especially in the weight room. Luckily head football coach, Del Elston, had no problem with me being there with the older players, even though I was years younger than everyone.

At the time, there wasn't an impressive training or weight room culture at Fillmore Central. I could count on one hand the players who lifted three times a week. My brother and I and a few players were the only regulars. Without much instruction or others to look to for my lifting, progress was slow. But though I was undersized and did not grow as fast as the other guys, I gradually got stronger and faster. From fifth to ninth grade, I was small but had a big work ethic. I soon became a starter in every sport I played.

As the years flew by, I continued to excel in sports. But though I was competitive, I wasn't physically growing. In fact, I was one of the last kids in my grade to hit puberty. At times, I would get made fun of because of how long it was taking for me to become a "man." But that never steered me away from sports. Nor did my size seem to bother my coaches, especially when they started calling up this undersized freshman for football, basketball, and baseball.

Even though I was waiting to have a growth spurt, it was completely out of my control, so I didn't let it slow me down. I stayed disciplined in the weight room throughout my middle and high school career and didn't let my height and size discourage me from working towards my goals.

In the end, it wasn't my crazy talents or gifted genetics, but rather my work ethic; my relentless drive to do things like sprint down hills and drag cinder blocks like a work horse. That's what propelled me forward. I was determined to do whatever was necessary to build my confidence, my constitution, and my capacity to grow both inside and out.

***

#OlstadsInsteads

Don't rely on talent alone. Instead, take the core fundamentals from your upbringing and apply an obsessive work ethic.

It was neither fancy nor was it the most proven technique, but I worked with what I had. And did it every day.

3

Sharpening Tools

To reach a goal, you must leave your comfort, certainty, and security behind in order to take a risk, but once you begin to take risks you realize that certain aspects of your journey are out of your control. You may think that you are limited because of your situation, but if you believe in yourself, you will realize that anything is possible. In life and in sports, you can determine your own level of commitment based on your goals and expectations. You set your own standard and the ceiling for your own potential is created within. If you create a routine of self-discipline, you can capitalize on factors such as your training regimen, positive energy, or diet that are within your control, and these become your "controllables."

Throughout my high school years, I became increasingly focused on football. My mindset shifted. I grew ever-more motivated to move forward, to take chances, and attain the next level. By the time I reached the latter half of my senior year, everything I did was a conscious step towards The Future. Those four years were a period of refinement. But that growth did not come without the pain that always accompanies change.

I wasn't the most popular guy in school and, at times, I struggled in the classroom. My parents rarely let me stay over at other people's houses and sometimes I felt sheltered. Occasionally, I felt lonely, a reluctant outsider. But all of that noise faded when my cleated foot crossed the white line onto the football field.

Whenever I felt excluded and had nothing better to do, I would work out my restless frustration by training and thinking about tomorrow. It wasn't normal to have such a routine, but those times helped develop my sense of discipline. Like sharpening tools on the farm when there's nothing else to do, it prepared me for my next game.

At times, when I didn't have classmates to hang out or train with, I always had my brother at home and he became my first mentor. Four years older, Levi and I bonded playing in the backyard. Much of that time he spent beating the crap out of me, but we simply loved to compete. In fact, Levi is the reason I played fullback, the most violent position in football.

One Sunday, during the televised halftime of an NFL game, we were playing a quick round of backyard ball when Levi started yelling at me. He thought I was giving up.

Pointing to the number on his jersey he yelled, "take that anger out on me! Turn this "39" into "93!" It was an intense moment. I was smaller and four years his junior. I didn't stand much of a chance. But that day, during halftime, I learned how to hit twice as hard. I gave it everything I had, and left the yard sore, with a solid, memorable headache.

Levi was and remains a passionate athlete and coach. His energy has left a lasting impression on me. When he left for college, I thought that I wouldn't see him nearly as much. But he came home every weekend for my football games.

Sophomore Swivel

During my second year of high school, most of my field time was spent on the kickoff team. I was way too small for fullback or linebacker, but I could run. And I wasn't afraid to take full advantage of every second on the field. I was scrappy and had a reputation for playing through the whistle.

During a game in Onalaska, Wisconsin, the first kickoff sent the ball high in the air and all 130 pounds of me screaming down the field. The tackle was made fast, but the whistle was slow to blow, so I absolutely lit up my opponent. The hit was more or less a cheap shot, but what did I care, I played only one down a quarter and I needed to hit something. I ran off the field and there was my Dad smiling, "you better have your head on a swivel next kickoff," he said as I made my way to the sideline. That kid never got me back, but those words stuck with me on the football field for my whole career. Keep your head on a swivel. In football or in life, always look out for yourself. You never know who you can trust or who is coming after you.

Back then, this over-the-top brand of aggression was how I played every sport. During basketball season, on the b-team and some varsity as a point guard, I was quick at guard, a ball handler; often attempting passes few would try. However, I quickly found that my football techniques on the basketball court would not fly. Every time an opposing player tried to set a screen on me, I tried to run them over. Although I loved basketball, my rough style of playing the game did not translate well.

Football had become my passion and every day I looked for ways to improve. I was consistently lifting and training year-round, during each winter and spring sport.

The Weight Wait

After my sophomore season, I realized that I wanted to take the sport of football all the way, and I was ready to push my body to make that happen. The first time I became conscious of that willingness, I was sitting in the kitchen, the day after Christmas, with the family. As we were eating, Dad looked over and asked if I was planning to play college ball. I immediately stopped the arm carrying food to my face and answered, "Yep." Raising an eyebrow, he grabbed my small bicep, "You'll never play college ball, or even get the chance, if you're not up to 200 pounds by your senior season."

At the time I was 130 pounds, soaking wet. To think that I had two years to gain roughly 70 pounds was daunting.

"How do you expect me to gain that much?"

"Start eating like a horse and living in the weight room."

I knew I was undersized, but over the years I had outworked my competition through a combination of technique, tenacity, and a relentless will to win. I never felt undersized on the field, but I knew that 130 pounds was not going to cut it.

"Access what is within your control," Dad encouraged. And with that advice, I started eating two to three helpings at each meal.

Not only did I eat, I camped in the weight room and took on every sport high school had to offer, including pole vaulting and running both the 100 and 200 in track. They were all off-season training for my goal. I was determined to be a 200-pound senior.

By Summer, I was roughly 160 pounds. I was slowly becoming a man and finally hitting that growth spurt that my peers hit in middle school. People I had known my entire life did a double take when I walked in the room. It was like I grew a foot overnight; even I was surprised.

The part that people didn't see was my constant gorging to pack on more weight. I would go to bed most nights so full that I felt queasy. Do I recommend doing this? No. But at the time I had little knowledge of proper weight gaining techniques. I just dug in, more motivated than ever.

My metabolism was relatively high, so I still looked lean regardless of whether I ate two steaks, a whole pizza, or a box of Little Debbie's in one sitting. And my main source of energy (and post-workout drink of choice) was skim milk. This may be the Minnesotan-Midwesterner side of me, but I would use the milk like fuel for my workouts. Back then I would drink as much as I could before bed, so I didn't lose any weight sleeping. Milk was and remains a staple of my diet.

Every person I encountered who asked me about football during those days, eventually inquired about what supplements I took. My answer was always the same, none. Obviously, once I got to college, I added protein powder to my diet because it is a healthy option for any full-time athlete. However, there are countless supplements in the world that promise results, and although I believe that protein can complement your daily eating habits and training routine, you will never see positive results if you rest all of your hopes on magic powder. You will see results if you have a dedicated and consistent routine. But if you let your discipline slip, supplements won't keep you from falling.

After a year of dedication, I slowly got my weight up to 165 pounds. And these early results carried over to my role on the field. My junior year saw my first start on the varsity team. I played fullback on offense and linebacker on defense, as well as a variety of other special teams. We were a decent team and had average success. The year went by fast but all roads lead to senior year. Throughout that season of change, nothing was given to me, everything was earned.

As Fall and my senior year approached, I was finally closing in on 200 pounds. I had dedicated myself to training and the weight room. And I worked to become one of the best players and leaders on my team. But after all that behind-the-scenes effort and dedication to the game, I was not voted captain my senior season. And that perceived slight would come to motivate me like nothing else.

The 2012 version of me was bummed that I did not receive recognition. But I have since learned that if you are going to do something, do it for the cause.

Once I realized that becoming a better player

was a positive act that helped the team, I was able to let go of my weighty burden, and throw my new 200-pound frame towards, what Dad called, 'accessing what is within your control' – which at that moment was stepping up my training for both our senior season and the ultimate opportunity to play college ball.

Confrontation

It was finally time to play the game, the first of our senior season. In the four quarters that followed, I never left the field. I was the fullback on offense who sometimes ran the ball, but usually led the way as the lead blocker. On defense, I was still at linebacker, because the one thing I knew was how to tackle. Nothing fancy, just old-fashioned football.

In game one, during warm-ups, I was watching the other team while they were practicing a screen play. It was one of the few times the opposing team would line up in shotgun fashion. Later, during the game when I saw them again lining up, I started yelling, "Screen! Watch the screen!"

As the ball was snapped, I took off for the running back. I knew the quarterback was going to throw the ball his way. Sure enough, once the ball was in the air, I grabbed it and ran it to the house for a touchdown. The momentum was ours.

In the little corner of the world where I was raised, football was not based on an arrangement of X's and O's in a playbook, but on the simple, visceral will to win. And that collective desire was never more focused than when we played Caledonia.

That equally small-town Minnesota squad had

a long winning streak. Going into the game, we were 6–0 and ranked in class "1a" (smallest 11–man football class). Caledonia was ranked #1 in class "2a" (2nd smallest 11-man football class). This meant that we would never meet up with Caledonia in the playoffs. Still, we wanted this win more than anything. The conference championship was on the line. We refused to be intimidated.

We came out of the gates hot, taking the kickoff back to their 5-yard line. But denied a touchdown, we opted for a field goal. They knew what was on the line and so did we. The game quickly shaped up to be the most confrontational of my high school career.

Early in the second half we lost our number one running back to a broken leg. Injuries happen . . . and so does disappointment. We ended up falling short in a close, hard fought game.

Had we won it would have been a victory to remember. But the fact that we didn't, became another lesson I will never forget: One day we can steal the ball and dance into the endzone, then the next, push to the 5-yard line and be denied the goal. The lesson is simple. Things don't always go our way.

Taking to heart these many lessons, all these tools that for four years had sharpened me, I was ready to leave the farm and plow a whole new field.

Wanting Winona

I had just finished my senior football season and I was motivated to play college football, but I didn't have a lot of attention from colleges during the season. What college was going to take a chance on me? I had decent tape that highlighted big hits and blocks that I made over the past few years, as well as a lot of tackles. I had a couple Division 3 schools consistently calling my phone, but I had little interest paying so much money to go to school. In high school I was a decent student, but I didn't put a lot of effort into my studies. Therefore, I didn't have much hope for a D3, "academic scholarship." By the end of my high school career, I was very ready to get on with my life and I had a burning desire to be great at everything I did.

To say that I begged Winona State to look at me, would not be an exaggeration. I mailed them highlight tapes. Then emailed them. After a lot of time and repetition (just like training) the effort paid off. I got a call.

I grew up one hour away from Winona, MN. It was a popular place, where many kids from my school district went to college. Back in the day, my mother and her family lived in Winona. And Dad's childhood farm was just 30 minutes outside the city limits. So, it was a huge moment when the phone rang. My father spoke with the recruiter first, discussing my work ethic and career. Then Dad handed me the phone.

Today, kids interested in playing at the college level have a social media account with posts and video of their athletic efforts. But in 2012, highlights were not as easy to get to coaches. However, once the Special Teams coach and I talked, it was not long before they showed up at my high school.

During that visit, I got to meet Coach Cameron Keller. I was on top of the world. Keller and his assistant, two big timers from Winona State

University, were there to see me—Zach Olstad! With briefcases in hand, they were decked out in all black, WSU gear. I felt overwhelmed with the possibilities.

The tension with some of my peers was another story. I was the principal's son and my Mom worked at the school, so I wasn't the most well-liked guy in my grade, constantly being in the same building as family. I felt misunderstood. I had a vision that some didn't understand and how I portrayed it may have come off as arrogant, but to me it was simply an internal obsession with continuous improvement. You learn as you grow up that elevating to a certain level comes with opinions from others. If you let those opinions effect you, you will never get to where you're wanting to go.

I shared my excitement with my family and knew that I was on the verge of an opportunity that I had worked for. I knew that to achieve my dream of playing college football I would have to overcome feelings of self-doubt and put myself out there. My greatest successes have come not when I was being safe, but when I was willing to take risks.

That visit from the WSU coaching staff, in turn, got me an official invitation to visit the Winona campus. Just being there was an education. The first thing I saw when I arrived was another problem to tackle, a big one. I was surrounded by gigantic dudes. I literally looked like a boy, and they looked like men.

"Have fun riding the bench your whole Winona State career," a high school classmate once laughed in my direction. Admittedly, I was a bit undersized for a linebacker or fullback. But I believed in myself.

And at that moment, my view was what mattered. If your mind is set on a goal, but you live your vision through the lens of another, you will never find your direction – or destination.

On an official campus visit, each recruit has a one-on-one meeting with the head coach. Mine was with Coach Tom Sawyer, a legend at Winona State. From the moment I entered his office, to this day, he has treated me with respect. The Coach has always been there for me, though at the time, he probably laughed a little when I asked if there would be any scholarships offered.

Looking back, I realize I spoke too soon. There was no scholarship. I would not be getting athletic monetary assistance. But, as luck would have it, I was encouraged when the Coach added, " . . . if you prove yourself, scholarships can be earned."

Say no more, I thought, let's get to work.

That day my verbal commitment to the Winona State Warriors was sealed with a handshake. Officially, I would be a walk-on.

I was about to join a Division II football team with a good program, and still be close to home. In my eyes, I had it made.

Now, all I had to do was build on the foundational lessons that high school taught me ... and keep my head on a swivel.

***

#OlstadsInsteads

Instead of rushing the process, access what is within your control . . .

Trust the Process.

4

Rhythm of the Grind

Every April, college football has what they call, "Spring Ball." Actually, more of a Spring 'thaw', this annual process entails fifteen practices, off season lifting, and a few scrimmages with one final warm-up clash. That culminating game is an opportunity for the school, community, and coaches to get a preview of what the team will look like during the regular season. It is an occasion for the players to get comfortable in their new roles, or reassigned positions.

During Winona State's 2012 spring game, the game announcer introduced, as usual, the team's incoming freshman class. One by one, every freshman's name echoed in the stands as they walked onto the field to join the team. But oddly enough, my name wasn't called. In fact, I was left standing on the sidelines.

Approaching the man in charge, I asked why I had not been introduced. Apparently, I wasn't on the list. Immediately my name, hometown, and position were radioed up to the announcer. It was a little embarrassing and not the smoothest start to my Winona career.

Because I was a walk-on, I knew I was an underdog. But being forgotten and unlisted that day, gave me fire. I was determined for my coaches and teammates to get to know me. That Spring Game became my springboard.

I had one advantage. I grew up a Minnesota farm boy. Having plowed the stumps and ditches of my home field, I learned early on that nothing happens overnight. It was all a process, a daily grind. Effort was the key. Like all sports, it's the combination of body, mind, and the determination of a reliable, farm work horse that gets you down the field.

With that in mind I approached each practice, showed up for each meeting, with a fierce determination to own my position. The first step in the effort was to be patient and be willing to follow the old football axiom: "If you're not a leader on the bench, you won't be a leader on the field."

I knew going into my freshmen year that I would be redshirted, there was no doubt about that. Being redshirted means that you don't get to play in any conference or out-of-conference games. In turn, the season that you are redshirted does not affect your 4 years of eligibility. In college athletics, a player has 4 years of eligibility. What that means is that you have 4 years of collegiate competition with opponents, so being redshirted as a freshman didn't affect those 4 years of eligibility.

With all this in mind, I started my first year of college at 5'11", 205 pounds. Officially suiting up for the Warriors as a redshirt linebacker, I was ready to learn. Coach David Braun was my position coach. He was a tough teacher, and his mental strength was palpable. But he was relatable. I respected the coach, for he treated everyone—redshirt or not—fairly, as long as you gave it everything that you had. Our best linebacker, Ryan Gerts, was the one for me to emulate. He was among Winona State's finest athletes. So, setting my freshman focus, I fine-tuned my ears to Braun's instruction and I focused my sights on Gerts' example; if I was going to ride the bench, I was determined to become its leader.

The 'One-Eleventh' Commitment

It doesn't take long to realize that college players are big, fast, and strong and that the coaches really do swear. It was quite the change of pace from small-town, high school football. This proved to be true during my first season as a freshmen linebacker when I attempted to make a tackle. I missed the tackle and as I came off the field my defensive coach screamed in my ear his idea of a perfect form tackle ending with, "you're SOFT AS F***!" I can assure you, the message was loud and clear. Football will teach you everything you need to know about life. Every player gets beat at some point. I always think back to the motto, "1/11th." My college coaches used it religiously and it was plastered all over the Bills facilities in the Pros.

There is not a better description of football. Getting down to the short and sweet of it, you do your job, and count on the other 10 men on the field to do theirs. If you execute your task to the best of your ability, your team has a promising chance to win.

The point is that a team is only as good as its weakest link. A football team needs everyone, and everyone involved has a duty. Even if you're not the player participating in the big games, you must still give more than 100 percent. During practice, I was constantly running scout teams as a linebacker working against our starting offensive team. If I didn't bring my best effort every single day, I would get called out, as any player should.

"One-Eleventh" isn't just a statement about what happens on the field, though. It's also about the preparation for the field; practice, lifting, nutrition, yoga, taking care of your body. Be the best you can be, no matter what position you play on the field, or in life.

Roughly 30 freshmen came in with me during that first year, and roughly 15 stuck with it through their entire career. College athletics isn't for everyone. In fact, by the end of year one, I was so overwhelmed I thought it might not be for me. But the exhaustion, injuries and early mornings couldn't compare to my desire to prove myself.

My advice to kids with the desire to play at the next level is no matter how rough, see it through.

Moving to a new city, meeting new friends, teammates, and an intense coaching staff, was definitely a transition. But committing to a goal, then honoring that commitment and sticking with it, is the only way to achieve success. It's like a handshake; there is something about a firm grip that says, "this is my 1/11th promise, with this shake I display my strength and my commitment to follow through and do my part."

Prove that you are willing to sacrifice, to learn, grow, and stick with it. If you do, the scoreboard may fluctuate, but the odds will always be on your side. It's a lesson I learned the hard way.

Going Through the Motions

As the scout team linebacker, I spent an entire year getting run over by offensive lineman. It wasn't the most glorified spot on the team. I was at the bottom of the depth chart, at middle linebacker on defense, and I was beginning to think my high school classmate was right: "You'll never play."

During that last month of my first season, we were practicing in the Minnesota frigid cold. I was undersized compared to most of the players and that meant that every hit I took felt like, and sounded like, a whip was being cracked in the frozen air. Every clash added up, and as the Bowl Game and the year passed, I was feeling ready for warmth and comfort. But then came the off-season workouts.

Each day was tough but on Fridays we got after it more than ever, our strength and conditioning coaches called it "speed school." Garbage cans were placed out by the coaches, for the players who needed to puke, but I was determined not to be one of them. I made it through the first Friday without the trash can. But when the workout was over, I could feel my gut tightening up. My sweat turned cold. Exhausted from the session, I knew that I didn't have long to get out of the training area. I should have taken the can with me. And that was just the beginning of my day.

The routine of getting up before the sun to attend off-season training was followed by a full day of classes. That itself took some practice. On top of football, I was a double major, double minor, pursuing a degree in Education just like most of my family. I was majoring in Physical Education, Health Education, and minoring in Coaching and Adaptive Physical Education. This schedule kept me very busy and very broke.

I didn't have a job during most of my career, outside of my regular summer gig back home at the bus shed. Being a college athlete taking 18–23 credits every semester was no simple task. It required a complete commitment of my time, and I learned to limit distractions.

I worked my butt off the entire off-season and my coaches noticed, but I was still undersized compared to most linebackers. The likelihood that I would get playing time as linebacker was slim. I had plenty of room for improvement and needed to grow into the position. I wasn't as big, fast, or strong as many of the other players, but I could see myself finding a home on special teams. I had the energy and the will to do anything asked of me.

One of my main goals was to "make the bus." A team can only take so many players on the road; only about 25 offensive players and 25 defensive players can travel. And not being an important contributor to offense or defense early on, it was crucial to play a role on special teams. So "making the bus" was a way to display commitment. Showing up with intensity that off-season was proof of my determination to contribute, to secure a seat; "roll that extra mile" in order to improve myself and the team. I did everything I could to be visible, to never again be overlooked. I had one main goal: "make the bus."

But staying focused, motivated, wasn't always

easy. And let's be honest, I didn't always feel like getting on board.

During that year's spring ball, I played decent at linebacker, but I wasn't making plays that stood out, and truth be told, I wasn't having much fun. Throughout that season, I was in touch with my folks about possibly quitting the team. And some evenings I would drive home in the middle of the night to talk with them about it. I was slowly losing sight of my end goal. I felt like I was just going through the motions.

I was leaning towards throwing in the towel. And that was my intent when I walked across campus for what the team ironically called, "The Exit Meeting": the last coach/player face-to-face before summer break. As I neared the coach's office, I crossed paths with another freshman, Collin Corcoran, who started at middle linebacker as a freshman. He could tell, from my slow walk, that I was disappointed. And stopping me in my tracks, we had a conversation. Collin and I were much alike. We shared a quietness that was a vast contrast to our savage nature on the field and in the weight room. I confided that I was thinking about quitting the team. He slapped me on the shoulder, looked me in the eye and told me what I already knew, "stick with it!" I'm not sure if it was his tone of voice, or his determined look, but his message put my head back on its swivel.

In that moment, I stepped out of myself and considered all of the work I had put in, all the hours of sacrifice. That persistence, perspiration, and all those aches and pains were for a reason, my betterment. All that investment would be lost, if I did not stay the course and put all my sharpened tools to work.

Collin's slap on the shoulder snapped me out of it. I decided to stop going through the motions and turn the savage side of my nature back to "making the bus." I was able to once more see the goalpost up ahead ... but not from the angle I expected.

A Change of Perspective

When Coach Braun sat me down for that "exit" chat, I held my breath. He praised my efforts, then expressed his appreciation for me as a linebacker. Then he added, "but, it would be best for the team, if you moved to fullback."

Exhaling with a smile, thankful for Collin's slap on the shoulder, I was relieved. I didn't care what position I played, I just wanted my name on the roster, with an assignment where I was needed.

I had gone through a full year of learning in-depth defensive coverages, alignments, gaps, and techniques only to be moved to a new position on the offensive side of the ball—talk about a change of perspective!

Looking ahead, I was now in my favorite position, fullback. And, to my further surprise, I finished the year with my first ever 4.0 GPA. My freshman year was in the books. Summer was on its way. It was time to go back to the farm.

***

Throughout college summers, I shuttled between Winona and home to work at the bus shed. For seven straight summers, it was my job to clean the buses: two summers in high school, and five after. It was a dirty job, but my brother Levi and I did it together and we loved it.

I knew that I could make a nice chunk of savings at the bus shed, so I spent every summer at home. But through it all, football remained my number one focus. To that end, in between shifts at the shed, I still showed up in Winona, throughout the summer, for scheduled workouts. They were not mandated by the coaches, but the team's senior leadership made it clear that if we wanted to take the next step, we needed to show our solidarity and build not only our physique, but also the team's character and chemistry.

Other players thought I was crazy driving an hour each way, several times a week, but it was a priority for me, and my daily schedule proved it. I was going straight from a 6–8 hour day at the bus shed, to farming over my lunch breaks. Then, hightailing it to Winona to attend the team workouts.

It was exhausting balancing my nutrition and training schedule with the need to make money and help my family on the farm. But somehow, I found the rhythm of the grind.

Some jobs at the bus shed were harder than others. But if I had to pick, cleaning underneath a school bus was the dirtiest. Those yellow beasts always took a beating over the region's mostly gravel roads. The worst of it came during the harsh Minnesota winters, when the vehicle's undercarriage was continually plastered with a thick layer of frozen salt. This multi-season collection of mush would leave the buses prone to the ravages of rust. And the only way to combat that inevitability would be to lay on a creeper (a rolling body cart), slide beneath the bus, and use a pressure washer to blast away the build-up of gravel and guck.

Before diving under a bus for this tedious operation, I learned to put on beat-up shorts, a ragged t-shirt, and safety glasses—which would quickly cover with mud, blinding me. It would take an hour, sometimes two, before the job was done. Under there, you didn't have time to feel sorry for yourself, once that pressure washer started to blast, you were instantly soaked; covered in crud and mud.

Every bus in the Harmony fleet would eventually get jacked up for body and engine work, so there was no hiding your mistakes or laziness. These metal machines exposed to the ever-changing elements were prone to fatigue and rust, so the job was important for both safety and longevity.

By the time I got home, my hair was as stiff as cement, and the rest of me was a splatter of everything from gravel dust to Amish-buggy horse crap. Eventually, after a thorough shower and a snack, I was off to Winona for practice. Given a few weeks of this, I found the rhythm.

Other jobs at the bus shed included: wrenching the wheels on and off along with sanding the rims down by hand, changing the oil, greasing, painting, cleaning, scrubbing, disinfecting, mending seats, and completing final washes before the upcoming school year. But my favorite job was the rare occasion when I got to mow the lawn and watch my brother continue to work inside the bus shed. Good work brother! By the end of the summer Mark and Donna Scheevels' fleet of buses looked brand new and were back in shape for the upcoming school year. If those tasks didn't build character, at the very least they gave me a few stories to tell.

Moral of the story was that I grew up working manual labor jobs. If you can take pride in your work knowing that it isn't always glamorous, you can carry that work ethic into other aspects of your life. Being a fullback meant doing the dirty work. Putting others first, consistently sacrificing yourself, and smiling after a good day of hard work. You learn to leave your ego at the door.

"Welcome To College Football . . . "

Over the Summer, Coach Markgraf, our fullbacks coach, and a variety of team coordinators would FaceTime me to go over the offensive playbook, to make sure I was ready for the season. During one of these bi-weekly calls the offensive coordinator, Cam Keller, took note of how much weight I had gained and warned, "You better be able to move Olstad. You're also on every special team's depth chart as of right now."

Having jumped from 205 to 225 pounds over the break, made me even more eager for the season. I couldn't wait to hit the field.

My pre-game ritual before every game was always the same. Two hours before kickoff I would meet my family in the parking lot and hand my necklace to Mom. That good-luck-on-a-chain held two charms close to my heart: a football engraved with my number #40, and a metal nut from the floor of the bus shed, etched on each side with "OLSTAD". Mom would wear my special chain during every game of my career. And after the final whistle, its ownership would revert to me.

Within the first ten minutes of the season's first game, our opponent Bemidji State, launched the ball in our direction, and changed my life and career forever. On that play, our starting fullback was hit hard, and his leg snapped as he got rolled up on by an opponent.

As I watched the play from the sidelines, my heart sunk. Immediately our offensive coordinator turned to the bench to pick a replacement. The tension was thicker than the humid night air. Glancing between his options, he seemed to move in slow motion. Then, finally, his ball-capped head moved.

Three months before, I was at the bottom of the depth chart on defense. Now, with the coach's simple nod, this game-one freshman, became the starting fullback. Mentally, physically, I was in the best shape of my life. Though the opportunity was unexpected, my tools were sharp. I was ready to be The Work Horse.

***

That first offensive possession we drove down the field. When our coach called a counter at the 10-yard line, I finally got into the game. I'll never forget the play. With the counter called, I sprinted around the edge to take on the opponent's middle linebacker. We collided. He laid me out, but I hit just enough of him for our running back to sneak into the end zone. I've never been bull-rushed as badly as I was during that hit.

We lost the game in overtime, letting a 20-point lead slip away. Our starting quarterback and fullback were injured and out for the remainder of the season. At the next day's team meeting, Coach Keller called me out on the score-making play. "Welcome to college football, Zach Olstad." It was a dirty, necessary job. Someone had to do it. And I was ready.

That first season was hard but productive. Though, as a team, it did not go as well as we hoped, I nevertheless was growing, in every way. I was preparing myself in the off-season to be a machine. I ate and ate and I trained much more than required. Coach Keller, our offensive coordinator, was always honest with me every off-season and it was clear that the first season had good moments, but more moments to improve on. My weight went from 225 pounds to 250 pounds that off-season. The key to gaining weight is not about taste or comfort. The weight gaining became painful and uncomfortable but being consistent kept my weight and strength climbing. This off-season may be my best off-season to date. I was big, felt quick, and had more strength and power than ever. One thing that continued to stick out during fall camp and scrimmages was that it didn't hurt as badly to give or take hits as I was much bigger than I was during my first year of eligibility.

The next time I mustered the courage to bring up the word "scholarship," I wasn't disappointed. When I told Mom the news, she cried.

Was it the necklace she wore during my games that made it happen? I'm sure it had something to do with it. But when it comes down to where the bus tires meet the gravel, it wasn't a lucky charm that got me from Harmony to Winona. It was being a work horse and pushing through the rhythm of the grind.

***

Spring ball came and went, and it was time for

me to forget about school for a couple months and focus on work and football again. There were four things that I needed to do all summer: work, eat big, train hard, and study film. I was headed into my third year of college and my second year of eligibility for football.

In college, I experienced two years in which I felt dominant at my position on the field, and it was my redshirt sophomore and redshirt senior year of eligibility (my third and sixth seasons). My football career began to slowly take off after my second year. But football is a tough and sometimes violent sport and as a fullback, hits start to add up. I could rarely be kept out of any sport or any part of life while growing up. But all of the hours on the field and in the weight room led to a turning point that became one of the most trying aspects of adversity that I had to overcome throughout the latter half of my career: injuries.

***

#OlstadsInsteads

Instead of settling for your current position, take a risk. Lead from the bench until your number is finally called.

As an underdog, you must be willing to be a work horse.

5

Warrior Code

If you happen to be in Winona, on a Saturday in October, you will find most of the city residents headed towards Maxwell Field, the local football venue. If you follow the crowd and wander up to the stadium's glass-enclosed press box, you will see on the wall an image of a Spartan warrior, inscribed with a Greek phrase.

Before a Spartan soldier would leave for battle, his wife would hand him his heavy shield and announce, "Come home with it, or on it." Those ancient words embrace every outcome. Taking note of that all-or-nothing spirit, the phrase not only emblazoned on the wall of Maxwell Field, but stitched into the uniform of every Winona Warrior.

Every time we faced an opponent on the scrimmage line, we gave it our all and left nothing on the field.

And to keep that motto always in mind, just before entering and exiting the stadium, every player passed by a giant metal shield. When we headed to the turf to warm-up before the game, we touched it. And, after our battle was fought, when we left the field, we would each lay our hand in homage on the Spartan Shield.

With this all or nothing attitude in mind, I entered my second year of eligibility on the college field feeling better both physically and mentally. I was bigger than I had ever been, even bigger than most of the linebackers on our team. I went from being a 130-pound fart in the wind to a 250-pound train.

I had finally grown into the machine that I had envisioned all those years ago. After everything, I was finally hitting my stride as an all-or-nothing Warrior.

***

The first few games of the season, I began to play really good ball. And because I realized I was improving, an old problem reappeared—over-confidence. This confidence led me to think that no matter the opponent I would win the battle. Such firm belief sometimes was the cause of injury.

During our third game of the season versus The University of Mary, we were running out the clock, about to secure a solid victory, when I lowered my head to plow over a defender. It was the cherry on top, victory hit. I ran him over with everything I had, hoping that he never wanted to step foot on Maxwell Field again. But as he fell to the ground, I was overcome with excruciating pain running from the base of my skull down through my spine. It rattled my tongue for what seemed like an eternity.

I didn't tell anyone what had happened. I simply ran back to the huddle and, despite the pain, kept playing to finish the remaining minutes of the game.

Afterwards, I went to get my neck examined. The training staff immediately put me in a neck brace, then drove me to the emergency room where I had scans and x-rays taken. The results were not good but could always be worse; I had sprained my neck. It was jammed, crunched, due to that final hit where I had lowered my head.

The day after each game, there is a team meeting where the coaches run through the highlights, list improvements that we needed, as well as name a player from both offense and defense, as the week's MVP. Ironically that neck-busting match with University of Mary was the only time in my career I was named the offensive MVP.

I stood up in front of the team with a neck brace, feeling like Bobby Boucher from the movie *Water Boy*, unsure if I'd be able to play the next week. The whole room laughed when Coach Sawyer asked, "Rough night?" Everyone knew what happened in the game and found a way to make light of what could have been a career-ending injury.

The real pain didn't hit me until later, when I realized I had been in this situation before. In the backyard, just after my brother taught me how to hit with everything I had. Along with Dad's speech about keeping my head on a swivel. Apparently, we all have lessons we continually have to re-learn; my reminder ended up being a pain in the neck – literally. And I can feel it at the base of my skull, to this day.

***

Although real recovery time was not an option, I did miss one game due to my neck. And another, when I was knocked out cold by an opponent, running down field after a kickoff. Eventually, however, the message got through and I started using my head for more than a punching bag. I put it back on its swivel and started looking before leaping. But when I did pounce, I gave everything I had, and proved that I could not only take it—but give it.

Seeing my head adjustment, the coaches made a few, too. I never again played multiple special team positions. But ironically, I found myself part of a unique squad called 'The Shield." Basically, I became one of three players assigned to protect the punter as he lined up the ball and executed his kick. We were his living breathing Spartan Shield.

Being one of the three shield members was kind of a kick for me, because I was the lightest player on the squad. Though I was big at 245 to 250 pounds, I was small in comparison to the other two shield members; each were as tall as a mountain and as wide as a Sumo Wrestler. Although I was the cream filling between these two cookies, I was neither intimidated nor afraid to take a hit.

The remainder of the season I stayed healthy and saw a drastic improvement in my ability. I played well and the coaches were pleased. I was even voted onto the team's leadership council. As the season ended, and we transitioned into off-season mode, I felt ready for whatever lay ahead.

But what I didn't realize was that the hits were adding up quickly and before I knew it, I was in need of a shield.

The Third Year Turn

In the middle of the Spring Game, just prior to the start of my third eligible season, I lunged to block a defensive player. As I fell to the ground, my left arm crossed in front of my body, and I landed directly on my elbow. When it hit the ground, my entire arm went numb from my shoulder down to my hand. I didn't regain feeling in my arm for ten minutes.

Just like that I was out of the scrimmage.

The trainers were positive that my shoulder had separated, but also sure it had gone back into place. Nevertheless, they were concerned I had suffered a serious shoulder injury, which meant something inside may have torn.

A few days later, I went to work out. But when I raised my arm, I had zero strength. Every time I attempted a lift, I felt a sharp pain shoot through me. Something was wrong.

After informing the trainers, I once more went through both an MRI and x-rays. The results confirmed the obvious: a posterior labrum tear in my left shoulder. A fullback's number one job is to block. Without power in my left shoulder, I wouldn't be able to perform my job to my expectations. Dr. Dahm of the Mayo Clinic assured me that the injury was too significant to play productively, and Coach Sawyer agreed.

I was at the top of my game, ready for the upcoming season. But in a blink, my arm was in a sling. All of the physical and mental energy I had stored up for my goals and purpose, in an instant, was torn away with my shoulder.

I ended up in surgery with months of recovery ahead. I was given a medical redshirt. I wouldn't lose eligibility, but I would not be playing in the upcoming season.

Down Time, Upside

It was one of the toughest years of my life. It ate at me knowing how much effort I had put in. Missing the entire year of football was made worse knowing that friends on the field like Alan May and Spencer O'Reilly, would soon be graduating. Both on and off the field, we were brothers. My sense of separation was as emotionally draining as the physical therapy regimen for my shoulder.

As the season kicked off, I began to gain weight and not the healthy kind. My disciplined diet and general sense of determination disappeared. And the combination of it all left me easily agitated and bitter. I woke every morning to another Groundhog Day of physical therapy and even more painful bench-warming; unable to do anything but watch from the sidelines.

Football represented structure for me. Not participating in the games was difficult and a change of pace, but it didn't mean I couldn't have an impact. I found a way to serve and help others. To ease my pain, I served as the tight ends and fullbacks student assistant coach. By no means was I an experienced coach, but I understood the offense well and helped with the playbook, drills during practice, and technique for the younger players.

The amount that I learned about the game from

my new vantage point was huge. What I picked up from the coaches during my medical redshirt season helped me to see the game in a whole new way.

Fist Fight

My fourth year at Winona was complete, I was finally cleared to play after 12 months of physical therapy. I was eager for life to return to normal. I was back to eating healthy, working out like crazy, and growing my hair back out.

I was now entering my fifth year of school and my third season of eligibility for the Warriors. I was 240 pounds. We started off the season with a 3–1 record, setting up what was our biggest conference game with our rival, Minnesota State, Mankato.

With one loss in Division II, you can still sneak into the NCAA Playoffs, but with two losses your team is on thin ice.

When Mankato comes to town, there is no doubt the stadium will be full and the environment, hostile. The Mankato-Winona rivalry goes back a ways. Being that both schools are just a couple hours apart, every kid recruited to Mankato also gets recruited to Winona. Winona's one loss made the stakes in this old rivalry feel even higher.

The game was a fist fight. Mankato and Winona brought their best.

The first half of the game was tight and by the third quarter the game was tied 17–17 with seven minutes left. We were driving down the field, when one of my favorite plays was called. I lined up away from the tight end on the weak side and my job was to run a wheel route up the sideline. We were at the 20-yard line and in good position to score. Throughout my career this play was called maybe five times total. But rarely was it executed this close to the end zone.

Our quarterback, Jack Nelson, called the play in the huddle and I felt electrified. The ball was snapped and all 240 pounds of me took off like lightning. I wheeled up the field between the sideline and the blur of numbers, when I turned toward the quarterback mid-stride. I saw the ball headed my way before it escaped into the sun. With the sun glaring into my eyes, I knew that I couldn't let the opportunity slip. In a split-second I found the ball at the six-yard line and caught it in midair. It was a perfectly thrown spiral by our QB and it landed in the palm of my hands.

The whole moment went blank. The next thing I knew I was giving Cam Johnson, our receiver, a hug in the end zone.

I had scored my first collegiate touchdown. After all the hugs, high fives, and smacks on the helmet, we completed our point after attempt. And just like that we took the lead, 24–17.

By the fourth quarter, the game was knotted up at 31, with just seconds remaining. The game was now down to our kicker. If he sinks it, we win. If he misses, we head to overtime.

Whenever a game comes down to the kicker and a final field goal, the tension is palpable. Some take a knee; some wrap their arms around each another. A few turn away, close their eyes, and there are even those who pray. Throughout my career, I tried every one of those approaches, but this time it felt different. This was seriously, the big moment of a crucial game. Lose two games in Division II, and the playoffs are extremely unlikely. We needed this one!

Carter, our kicker, took the field with a confident stride. The snap was solid, our field goal team stood strong, and as the ball was in the air, time stood still. The referee's signals came up and the crowd erupted, Warrior fans screaming in joy.

The student section overflowed the field. It turned into a sea of Warrior Purple and the celebration ensued. We were now 4–1 and still in contention for the playoffs.

Gut It Out

We were approaching game six of the 2016 season, at Upper Iowa University. Before the game, we stopped at Luther College in Decorah, Iowa, for a team lunch. After one bite of pasta my stomach took a turn for the worst. I found myself hugging the toilet. From the moment I woke up that day, I felt ill.

I informed the trainers of what was going on and there was no doubt that I had been hit with the flu bug. I felt miserable during warm-ups and throughout most of the game, but I was determined to get by and do my job.

Puking and dry heaving on the sidelines, I looked up in the stands where my Dad and brother stood. They knew I was miserable but yelled "gut it out!"

I had to summon all of the energy and inspiration that I could muster in order to keep going. I thought about Michael Jordan, when he famously played through the flu during the playoffs in 1997. His will to win led him to scoring 38 points, bringing his team to a 90–88 game five victory over the Utah Jazz. I knew that I had to keep pushing.

I managed to get through most of the first half when, just before halftime, another defining moment arrived.

Moments before halftime a run play was called. I climbed to the linebacker and hit him at a side angle to ensure a good edge for our running back. Doing so, my plant leg gave out and my ankle caved to the outside. I felt a pop and immediately knew that my foot had just snapped. I could barely walk into the locker room.

At halftime, the training staff checked my foot and ran some tests. They assured me it wasn't too serious. "If your foot was broken, you wouldn't be able to bear this test." They then smacked around my ankle and had me hold it in certain positions against their force. And here I thought that puking up my lunch would be the worst part of my day.

I played the second half, powering through the pain and we went home with a victory.

Two short days later, x-rays revealed I had a broken foot. My fifth metatarsal, the long bone on the outside of my foot that leads to the pinkie toe, had snapped. My foot was broken, and we still had five games left in the season.

Our upcoming game was against another solid opponent in Sioux Falls and it was our homecoming. I was so sick of injuries at this point that I asked the doctor what I could do to play through the injury. I was told that if I could get the inflammation down, that I may be able to play with less pain but that

I would need to have surgery as soon as possible.

I tried everything within my power to alleviate the inflammation in my foot before the homecoming game. I taped my foot and ankle in different positions and took anti-inflammatory and pain medication, but nothing helped relieve the pressure or pain. I played in the homecoming game but being on the field with a broken body part felt like a bad dream. Moving laterally made me want to fall to my knees. I wasn't myself with the broken foot, but I was getting by and still performing well enough to stay on the field.

We lost the homecoming game that season, and my thoughts spiraled. At night in bed, I would stare at my ceiling and wonder if I was coming home with my shield, or on it. Then I remembered what my father said when I came home after my first sports injury, "It's a long way from your heart." And my heart was still in the game.

Going into the Augustana battle, there was still hope for the playoffs or a bowl game. But if we lost this one—game over.

The fight was fierce. We were neck and neck every quarter. And like our earlier tussle with Mankato, it all came down to one last play: a Hail Mary pass, that was called "incomplete."

Feeling like the refs had missed the mark on the Hail Mary play, was difficult. We finished the season 8–3. We didn't receive a bowl invite and definitely were not going to the playoffs. Our team was broken, three games that season came down to the last play of the game. Every single game had been do or die.

I had a lot of decisions to make following that

season. The teammates that I had started with in 2012 had finished their last season and were done. But I had one more year of eligibility, due to the year I was redshirted for shoulder surgery. I had finished the season with a broken foot and would soon be enduring another surgery. Along with my foot I had a knee that had significant cartilage tearing. My shield was looking more like my stretcher.

Following the season, I had my second surgery in back-to-back years. Afterward, I wore a walking boot for a month, but my pain was not subsiding. I received x-rays and it was clear that my foot was not healing correctly. The x-rays showed two separated bones with a gap between them that looked like the Grand Canyon, and one screw drilled through each bone, holding them together. They put my foot into a hard cast for another month hoping the bones would fuse.

No signs of healing were happening, and the clock was rapidly ticking, I couldn't afford to miss another season.

Looking for a second opinion, I went back to the Mayo Clinic where I had my shoulder fixed. There, I was told that my best bet would be to start over and go through another foot surgery. At that moment, I could see my own exhaustion mirrored in the faces of my parents. I informed the doctors I would not be opting for the surgery.

I started different physical therapy programs to strengthen my foot before my final season arrived. The doctors were concerned that at any time I could step on my foot wrong and snap the screw holding the two pieces of bone together. If that happened another surgery would be required, and my career would be over. It was a risk, but one I was hell bent to take so I could finish my final season.

With effort, I finally got to a stage where my foot was in less pain and once more began intense training. I was ready for any off-season workout and attended every training session possible. The risk was high as my screw and foot could re-break at any time, but I had to train up to my standards. Otherwise there was no point in playing.

Off-season workouts were going well and my senior season was looking promising. Of course, in the back of my mind I was worried about my foot, shoulder, and knee, but I couldn't let fear override my focus. I was one of the sixth-year seniors that upcoming season.

Mike Imperiale understood my perspective. A linebacker from Illinois, we both came to Winona State as freshman in 2012. We both had been through the highs and lows of the game and had our fair share of injuries. Without Mike, that last year would not have been nearly as memorable. And for us both, that season did not begin on the field. It started back home, on my farm.

As one of the leaders on the team, every summer I had a group of 25-plus players out to my folk's place, an hour drive from Winona. It was a great excuse to have some fun before the fight and connect with each other. What better place to cultivate a sense of teamwork than on a field where things grow—which was my pitch to Mike.

He was one of the best players on the team, but the city boy from Illinois required a little coaxing to come out to the farm. Eventually "Mikey Mo' Cheddar," as his teammates called him, gave in.

We had a ton of fun. Mom and Dad turned each meal into a feast. And given the size of our group, we managed to drink my hometown liquor store dry. It was a great bonding bash, and rare time to get each other's perspectives on the upcoming season.

Going for a ride in my parents' Ranger, Mikey and I spoke openly about our anxiety. We both knew we would have to play a higher caliber of ball to win the games that would get us to the playoffs. We were aware that our Warrior offense was playing one kind of game and the defense was often playing another. And in the course of our long conversation, we realized that it would take our combined voices to mend the fractures between us. It would require the constant reminder of our "1/11th" promise to truly be a single fighting force. The only way to win this last shot was for us all to rally behind the same shield. Coming up with a plan for our one more opportunity, I offered up an old farm-ism, "The hay is in the barn!" This basically meant we've completed our summer training. It was all in the storehouse. Now it's time to put up or shut up.

Warrior Code

For the past five seasons, I have run towards the battle carrying the sentiment of the Warrior shield. I have served on a special protection squad that personified "The Shield." And given my many injuries, I have even been written off and on the verge of being carried away on that shield . . . But this Warrior was not defeated yet. As a team, we had one more shot to go big or go home—to return from battle with our shield, or on it.

The four captains nominated for the 2017 fall

season were Mike Imperiale (LB), Andrew Spencer (S), Nick Pridgeon (LB) and Zach Olstad (FB). I had never felt more prepared for what lay ahead. My off-season training program, nutrition plan, and recovery regimen had worked together to make me the fastest and fittest of my college career.

We had a great defense, talent in our special teams, a solid run game on offense, and a pass game that could take the top off our opponent's defense. We were destined to do something special.

***

We started off the season 8–0. Our first and only loss in the regular season came to our old rival, Minnesota State, Mankato. We finished the season at home against our worthy adversary, Augustana. If we beat them, we would clinch the playoffs for the first time in 10 years.

As team leaders, Mikey Imperiale and I met a few days before the game to talk about the significance of the moment and what was on the line. Sitting with him, reminded me of our time back on the farm. There, we found our focus and worked together to heal the fractured factions of the teams two sides. The Offense and Defense were now in sync, in tune, and on the same page. Now it was just a matter of mapping out the strategy and mustering the strength.

By the end of our pow-wow, we were both stoked, and simply happy for "One More." In hopes of that outcome, the day before the big game we bought a few cases of beer, a couple bottles of champagne, and some celebratory cigars for the locker room.

The game was set for a Thursday night in

Winona. To say it was going to be some serious football weather would be an understatement. At game time the temp was 20 degrees and quickly dropping, with a negative windchill.

From the moment the coin was tossed, until the fourth quarter end, we set the tempo and embraced the cold. We took the opening kickoff to the house for a touchdown. We made our opponent tap out within the first quarter and finished the game with a 52–21 victory.

The celebration was like no other feeling I've ever had on a football field. Our ten-year drought was over, and we were heading to the playoffs. We would finally have the opportunity to play for a National Championship. I'll never forget the tears rolling down my face.

Walking into the locker room with cigar-lit smiles, frozen from the raw Minnesota weather, we showered each other with champagne. In that moment, everyone was howling and laughing in an explosion of sheer joy; remembering with appreciation every second of hard work, every moment of pain we endured separately and together. It was a pure and perfect moment that will never be forgotten.

Eventually everyone made their way out of the locker room, but me. Sitting on the bench still in my uniform, I didn't want the moment to be over. I had just experienced over fifteen years of lessons as an athlete; in the classroom and on the field. And despite the countless injuries, or because of them, it had all paid off. The satisfaction, the emotion, the clarity of it was like nothing I've ever felt.

The Winona State Warriors eventually outscored its opponents in the 2017 season 400 to 175, and we finished with a record of 10–2.

***

I'll forever be indebted to the program that gave a kid from the middle of nowhere a shot at walking on and making the most of his career. Most importantly, I am thankful for the teammates, lifelong friends, and brothers that I made along the way.

I eventually took my nameplate off of my locker, left the locker room and found my family for one last round of post-game hugs. Then, with my friend Cale Stensgard in tow, we all took a slow, final walk off the stadium field. And as we passed the hanging Spartan Shield, I paused, and gave it a tap, one last time.

***

#OlstadsInsteads

Instead of throwing in the towel, know the difference between pain and injury...

And come home with your shield.

6

Porch Pacin'

I was back on the farm, but my mind was far from it. At least that's what I thought ... My agent said that if I was going to receive good news, it would come a day or two following the NFL draft. So, the day after the big event, I was on my feet early, walking my parent's front porch, alone. Waiting. Worried.

I was 24, four years older than most of the players being drafted into the NFL. My savings were gone. No job. Drowning in student debt. To say I had some concerns, would be putting it lightly. But as I paced that lofty hillside porch, the vista of our family's little slice of heaven seemed to quiet the impatient clock ticking inside my head.

Before my last season of college football, the doctors recommended that I hang up my cleats. Considering my back-to-back surgeries, the diminishing cartilage in my knee, and the screw in my foot barely holding together my bones, it was the consensus that I should just walk away. Or, as the doctors implied—hobble off the field. Naturally, I didn't listen.

Now, gazing at the farm from my family porch, I knew the clock had run out on my college career. But I wasn't ready to throw in the towel just yet. Instead, I was pacing, reminiscing, waiting for the phone, ready to hear the news ... about what? My shot at pro football, of course.

As usual everyone knew I was a long shot, and that I would be risking everything. But the work horse in me still had plenty of fields left to plow.

***

In order to give myself the best shot at the next level, I first spoke to the one man who had been with me through every quarter of the last six seasons.

I knew that Coach Sawyer's advice would be truthful, and that his direction would chart for me the most accurate path to my next end zone.

I sat down in his office with great pride in my collegiate career. I laid my cards on the table and told him I wanted to chase my lifelong dream of playing at the next level. Whether I made it to the CFL (Canadian Football League) or NFL (National Football League) or no league at all, I wanted to, at least, give it a shot.

Keeping in mind that not one NFL or CFL scout had inquired about me, and that I had 30 documented injuries spanning the last 6 seasons, the coach gave it to me straight, "it's a long shot." All things considered, I left the meeting with a glimmer of hope. Coach told me he would do his best to arrange a spot for me in the upcoming NSIC Pro Day. Coach Sawyer was a man of his word.

To get ready for this challenge, I put Englebert Training Systems (ETS) into my schedule; a facility specifically designed to accelerate an athlete's skills. There, I prepared for my Pro Day performance. It was a big risk; with over $35,000 of student loan debt, no savings, and less than $200 to my name, it was crazy. But I had to go for it.

So, I set a new rhythm to the old familiar grind. Every Monday and Tuesday I would spend at the ETS training facility, Wednesdays back in Harmony working the farm, and finish out the week at ETS before returning to Amish Country for the weekend. During those five months my body, and my truck, both racked up their share of miles.

While chasing this dream, I noticed that many players in my situation were hiring an agent; a rep to help get the attention of NFL scouts. So, I contacted a few agencies. Of course, they had no idea who I was. Most of them told me plainly, "You won't make it." One agent who told me flatly, "You have no shot. Not interested," eventually took on a few of the guys I trained with at ETS. None of them made it.

After some searching, I finally found Team IFA, based out of Minneapolis. The only catch was, being I was a nobody, I had to pay a monthly fee of $300 for them to work with me. That, added to my food, gas, and ETS training fees, shrank my bank account past nothing.

But having an agent was important. Their task was to make sure that the NFL and CFL knew I existed. But privately, Team IFA made sure I knew that promoting a fullback from a D-II school was not going to be easy. The "fullback" position was the least sought-after in both the American and Canadian leagues. And, if that wasn't enough bad news, the CFL also restricted the number of American players on their team. But I had to try every angle, travel every road possible... So, I decided to try out for the Canadians.

Rabbit Trails

Though I was a month away from the NFL Pro Day opportunity Coach Sawyer had secured for me, I decided on a whim to try out for the team north of the border. The irony of it was that my audition for the Winnipeg Blue Bombers would be held in, of all places, Arizona.

In February its always cold, on both sides of the northern border, but in the American southwest, terms like 'winter' and 'cold' can be better described in one word, 'HOT!" To this kid from Harmony, who had never even been on a plane before, landing in Arizona was like stepping onto the surface of the sun.

The tryout was being held at an old high school. And it felt like the scouts in the stands were there solely to collect our $100 entry fee. Despite the heat of the day and the cold reception of the scouts, I was determined to give it everything I had.

My performance during "the gauntlet" caught the eyes of the scouts. It was a test of speed and ability. Quarterbacks would line the field, allowing players to sprint between them, catching each of their passes consecutively. The scouts were surprised that a fullback of my size could run and catch like I did.

Drills, like the gauntlet, are designed to see if a player will go all out. You don't jog in football. I went as fast as I could and not only caught every ball but also every eye. All I needed to do was hold onto that momentum.

There were about ten minutes left in the tryout and the last drill was one-on-one routes versus defensive players. During my last attempt, I made a quick cut to gain separation from my defender. That's when I felt my knee lock, and I was headed down, fast. I hit the ground hard. And to my horror I heard a subtle pop from my knee. Here we go again . . .

With all of my weight I landed directly over my warped leg. A stab of pain instantly shot through my body. I knew something was wrong.

Somehow, I hobbled back to the huddle and finished the last ten minutes the best I could. Afterward, two of the scouts approached me. I could sense their interest. I remember one scout telling me that if I was Canadian, they would have signed me on the spot. Unfortunately, I was just an American, suffering the disappointment of being both a 'non-skill' position fullback (which the CFL doesn't normally sign) and a perspiring Minnesotan with a bum knee.

Once I got back to my Arizona pad, my throbbing knee began to swell. I got onto the floor to stretch, hoping that it was just a strain or a cramp. But as I sat back in a kneeling position, I heard my knee pop again and felt it immediately lock. I was stuck on the floor in agony, and nobody was there to help.

After several failed attempts to unlock my knee, I finally found the right angle; bending my injured left leg to the side as I grabbed my ankle inward. I felt my knee slowly unlock. That torquing movement helped my knee finally release.

I was terrified that I had ended my career one month before my NFL Pro Day while trying out for a Canadian team. Two days later I was at the Mayo Clinic in Rochester, MN for an MRI. The procedure is uncomfortable. But what makes it even more irritating is the machine's tomb-like shape. As I laid in that claustrophobic tube, countless questions ran through my head. Was my career over? Had I really come this far to once again be tackled by another injury? But one steady thought put my head back on its swivel—this was nothing I hadn't been through before. I had to find a way to move forward.

The MRI results showed a partially torn LCL (lateral collateral ligament) and a complete lateral meniscus tear. The doctor warned that the LCL could be completely torn with one wrong move-ment—like an aggressive lateral cut on the football field. The Doc stressed that both injuries would have a lengthy recovery time following surgery.

I had just one month until my NFL Pro Day. If I was going to get in front of the scouts, surgery wasn't an option.

I told my doctors that I wanted to keep these new injuries off my medical records so it wouldn't raise any red flags. They told me that there was no way my knee could handle the Pro Day stress, especially so soon. If I went back to training it would be against medical advice. The choice was mine.

Seeing my determination, the doc reluctantly recommended a knee brace, in case the LCL gave out. He said it could avoid total knee damage. But I couldn't even afford gas, let alone a thousand-dollar brace. Besides, wearing such a thing to an NFL Pro Day was out of the question. In the NFL, if you are hurt you are cut, that's how it works.

So, I had to risk it all, again.

For two straight weeks, I iced and elevated my knee and only did upper body exercises. Was it ideal? No, but it was the hand I had been dealt—or should I say, the knee.

Go Hard or Go Home

After the two weeks, I returned to ETS to finish preparing for my NFL audition. While training, I wore a light compression sleeve on my knee and went for it. I was far from 100% but I didn't feel sorry for myself. Learning which positions would lock up my knee took some painful practice. The only thing I couldn't control was lateral movement. It could finish the tear. My only option was to keep moving ... forward.

The day finally arrived. The excitement was real. My nutrition and training were on point, and I was ready to go. The long tights I wore to hide the compression sleeve on my bad knee, was the only reminder I needed that this ... was ... it.

There were roughly twenty players from the NSIC conference invited to that Pro Day. And of all the players on the field, I had the least amount of college statistics, least number of fancy awards, and drew the least attention in college. But no one there had more fight.

Like Arizona, the event was far from what I expected. I had dreamed of walking onto the field and being swarmed by every NFL team asking for my name. But when I showed up, it was almost comical. Only three scouts were there, representing The Colts, Bears, and Vikings. But three was better than none!

The day started with the bench press; where each player attempted to press 225 pounds as many times as they could. Next, the vertical jump, measuring how high one can fly. Then the broad jump, where the players were gauged on distance. Each participant cycled through, and their results were recorded. Then came the 40-yard dash and other speed events, such as Pro Agility (5-10-5), L-drill, and exercises that were position specific.

These drills were somewhat predictable and have been used for years to judge the core assets of a player. However, what these drills do not reveal is what is on the inside. Character is hard to judge, especially given the short four hours of a Pro Day.

That day I tackled each test by relying on my farm bred fundamentals. I pushed my body as if I were climbing the steep hills back home. I powered through every obstacle the way I once dragged those cinder blocks through the high grass. Those long-ago yard lessons had carried me to this all-important day. And knowing this moment could be my last opportunity, I flexed every muscle of my training.

All of us Division II hopefuls knew our chances of being drafted were low. For us to make it or even get a shot, we would have to strain like a work horse pulling a plow through a hard, dry field. I knew that my Pro Day results would be consistent, dependable. But would the effort be enough?

***

I was finished, but was I done? I had tried every

angle, explored every rabbit trail, and even attempted a few things that, looking back, now seem impossible. I had planted the seeds, tended the field, harvested the crop, and even put the hay in the barn.

All I could do now, is pace the porch . . . and wait.

**

#OlstadsInsteads

Instead of stressing about things that are no longer in your control, remember the windmill...

"If you're foundation is firm, the same storm capable of blowing you down can become the fuel that keeps your wheel spinning, pumping, and productive."

7

The Call

There is no reward without risk. I would have been discontent if I had never pursued my dream, but I knew that I could be satisfied if I fully dedicated myself to this journey. If I wasn't willing to put in the work, this would have been a wasted opportunity. I did not want to wonder what could have been or feel regret that I never tried, and I felt that great failure was better than uninspired success. Playing football was something that I loved like nothing else, and I wasn't pursuing the NFL for the money or the hype. Until I was left with no news or bad news, I was raised to believe in myself and the process. After many years of disciplined training, the road led to waiting on one call.

When I woke up on the morning of April 29, 2018, everything was quiet at my parent's house. I grabbed a cup of coffee and went to the porch to sit with the dogs while I collected my thoughts. Soon after, the morning tranquility transitioned to restlessness. I threw on my workout clothes and jumped into my truck, pointing it towards my old high school. The 2018 NFL draft had ended the night before, and it was the biggest day of the year for undrafted and tryout hopefuls like me. I will never forget that morning's drive into my high school weight room. Most Sundays I would have been in church, but my agents had told me to keep my phone on loud in case I received a call, so I spent that morning at the other place that I found peace. I had driven that same gravel road en route to the school thousands of times, and that day it felt nostalgic and surreal. Over the years I had lost friends, girlfriends, and time with my family because of my deep obsession to perfect my passion of football. I knew that it could be my last trip into the school to train for this goal, and every pothole and pole shed along the way made me reminisce.

Throughout my life, I had spent long hours in that dark, quiet basement, transforming into the athlete I had envisioned myself to be. Over the years, the culture in the weight room has grown. When I started lifting, it felt like it was just me and my brother, and now it is a staple of every sport's program at the school.

I arrived at the school, parked my truck, and made my way into that hallowed dungeon. After flipping the lights and the radio on, I began to warm up. I couldn't help but feel overwhelmed. Every song that came through the speakers hit a different note and spoke to me on another level that day.

I didn't train insanely hard that morning which was unusual for me as I always tried to push my body to its limits. I was doing some light bench presses when I looked up to the ceiling and thought to myself: if this is going to be the last time in here, why shouldn't I leave my mark. I took a pen from the weight room desk and climbed up the squat rack to write, "one more," on the ceiling. For me, the expression "one more" is meant to encourage others like me, working as hard as they can, to pursue one more opportunity.

I was lost in thought, feeling that something special was coming. Within an hour of being in the weight room, my phone started blowing up with texts, one right after the other.

Approaching my phone, I could see capitalized text and once I got to my phone I saw my agent's name and the classic saying, "HOLY SHIT DUDE," followed by, "The Buffalo Bills are calling in 10 minutes, have your phone on you!"

I called my agents in disbelief of their texts. They answered immediately and said, "Hang up now, they could be calling any minute."

I can still feel the moment in that weight room as chills, sweat, and tears overcame me. Physically, I felt like I was floating, hearing nothing but the silence in the room, as I made sure my phone was "ON" and completely charged. I felt a little charged, too—like the blurred vision you get when you aren't sure if you are seeing clearly or not.

For those ten minutes waiting on their call, time stood completely still. I swear I looked at the clock a thousand times and not a minute went by. Tears of joy and tears of pain rolled down my face off and on until I could get my heart rate down. Then I had a better idea, I thought to myself maybe I should leave the dungeon and find a place in the school with better service. I left the weight room and started pacing the hallways where I once attended class. Trying to keep my distance to avoid any conversation with anyone who might be in the school, I continued to pace.

Finally, as I looked down at my callused, sweaty hands, the sound of my phone reverberated throughout the hallway. As I picked up, I heard a voice on the other end, "Hello is this Zach?" "Yes sir," I said. "This is Brian with the Buffalo Bills and you're invited to our rookie minicamp," he said as if it was just another day on the job.

"Thank you for the opportunity sir, I appreciate it." I paused and didn't hear anything on the other end, so I asked, "What is my next step for getting out to Buffalo?"

"Everything will be sent and communicated with your agents. Be ready to go and come prepared," he said, winding down the call.

"Yes sir, thank you again," I said, and we both hung up.

To myself I thought... that was quick. To him I probably sounded dumbfounded, but that's how I felt after finally getting to see my dream come to life.

I couldn't wait to call my parents.

My Mom answered after one ring and sounded nervous after she heard that I was out of breath, but it wasn't from training this time. I told her to come to the school as quickly as possible and bring Dad, and then I hung up the phone.

Our farm is less than ten minutes away from the school and that is exactly how long it took them to pull into the school parking lot. I quickly set up my phone as I heard them opening the school door, just up the stairwell from the weight room, and recorded their reaction as I told them the news.

In the video, you can see me start the recording as my parents neared the door. My Mom walked in assertive and concerned. My Dad came in slowly behind her, relaxed but apprehensive. I didn't have much time to plan what I wanted to say or how I would say it but I knew that no matter how it came out it would be authentic.

As they were looking at me with all of the wonder in the world, I started to clap. When I finally found words, all that I could get out was, "Buffalo Bills." My Mom and Dad both locked eyes and perked, shocked. After their brief gaze of disbelief, my Dad said it even louder for my Mom and I to hear, "The Buffalo Bills ... Zach's headed to the Buffalo Bills!"

Overcome with emotion, my Mom started bawling as my Dad brought it in for a bear hug. Sharing the news with them is my favorite moment of all time. Everything that I did was for my family, and they had done everything they could to support me, every step of the way. Whether I ended up getting two days in the NFL or more, I was 24 years old and I had reached the biggest goal of my lifetime.

I enjoyed the moment with my parents before calling my brother who was at church with his wife and kids. He knew that I was waiting for news and left the church service when he saw that I was calling. I could hear the pride in his voice as he broke down once I told him. Levi had been my mentor and idol from day one, and all I could think was, "turn this 39 into 93!" I then called my sister who was at work in Austin, TX.

There is nothing better than sharing good news with the people you love most in the world. They knew that this was not just for me, but that it was for all of us.

Coaches, friends, family, and people who have helped me along the way were called, and then it was right back to work.

My weight was roughly 240 pounds that day and I knew that I had never been more dedicated in my career. Those months of training prior to the call changed my body into a finely tuned machine. With how short rookie minicamps are, I knew that I wouldn't have much time in Buffalo to make an impression. But even if it would just be a day or two in the NFL, it was the opportunity that I had worked for my entire life.

I had eight days at home before heading to Buffalo for the tryout. During those days, I traveled up to train at ETS Performance and each night my parents would grill and cook healthy and hearty meals for me to keep my weight up. My focus was complete; the way I felt when I walked on the Winona State field the first time—I had nothing to lose.

Yes, I had a few current injuries including turf toe, a partially torn LCL and lateral meniscus tear in my left knee, along with broken sesamoid bones in my feet, but I was feeling very ready to compete and nothing was going to hold me back.

"One more" is what I had earned. But one more of anything might not be enough to satisfy.

To make an impression I had to be perfect and exemplify every tool I had acquired from my upbringing. I had one chance to prove to the Bills, that if they put me in their harness, I'd be their Work Horse.

***

#OlstadsInsteads

You don't need a lot of people. Instead, all you need is a small circle who have your back.

"No one reaches their greatest moment, alone."

When your dream comes to mind, who is in the huddle with you? Whoever shows up, let them know how grateful you are and that you, too, have their back.

8

One More

NFL rookie minicamp was not the average job interview. It was my final opportunity to experience that ol' feeling of "one more."

When you know that you only have 72 hours to make an impression, every asset has to be at the ready—full throttle. Complete fearlessness, absolute exertion, mental visualization, are all necessary. But it is not enough to be physically prepared for the scrimmage line, it is important to also portray championship character both on and off the field.

On May 10th I left for Buffalo, New York. Arriving at my gate, I recognized another player from my college conference. Though he too had received an invitation to the rookie minicamp, he looked as if he was on his way to an interview with a financial firm. I got a kick out of it and thought to myself, either he overdressed or I sorely underdressed. I knew that I probably looked a little raggedy at the time, as my shoes were worn with holes and the sweatpants that I was wearing were a pair that I've had since high school. I had invested my last dollar into training, nutrition, and agent fees along with several trips to the chiropractor and physical therapist appointments. I had put it all on the line, and then some, and I was ready to put my body on the line as well.

When we arrived at the facility, the first person I recognized was the running back's coach, Kelly Skipper. We had never met before, so I approached him and shook his hand like I meant it. A firm handshake and direct eye contact was giving him my "1/11th Commitment." Recognition is a sign of respect, and a quick way for coaches to remember you, even in a short time.

Following my talk with Coach Skipper, all of the rookies filled out paperwork on past injuries. My list was a red flag, if not a complete deal breaker. We were to detail our entire history of surgeries, injuries, and concussions; a task that would have taken more time and far more paper than I had. So, I keyed in a couple of the significant injuries that I had endured throughout college, keeping to myself the results of the CFL tryout and my freshest wounds.

I was used to carrying on despite injuries. Some did not understand why I was so hell-bent to continue, but I knew that I had much more to give. I was confident that no matter what physical pain I experienced, I could get through it. Nothing had slowed me down, yet.

Of course, I was not expecting to play football forever. I knew my list of injuries was a ticking clock. But I was determined to keep going – all the way—right up to the final whistle.

***

After Coach McDermott addressed the room of

rookies on the particulars of the 3-day protocol, their expectations, and the standards of what being a "Bill" entailed, we were handed our rookie playbooks and dismissed. As we were leaving for the hotel, I noticed Coach McDermott standing in the doorway. Seeing no better opportunity to introduce myself, I approached him, nodded, and put out my hand, "Coach, my name is Zach Olstad, I play fullback." Shaking my hand, in return, with a firm grip he grinned, "You look like a fullback ... I love it."

The rookies were shuttled to two different hotels, a run-down motel for the tryout players, and a hotel full of suites for the drafted/undrafted rookies. Upon arrival, a lot of the guys were making friends and plans for the rest of the night. I had little to say to anyone. We were not here to have fun but to get the job done.

The first night, I left my roommate behind and began my prep in the hotel lobby at 7pm. I poured over that playbook front to back until 3am. Our wakeup call was set for 6am. I didn't think that I would be able to sleep anyway. The steam from my coffee continued to roll as I looked around and there was no one in sight besides the lady at the front desk, who looked at me with a confused expression. I wouldn't go to bed until I was confident in both my assignments and the assignments of everyone around me. I needed to find my competitive edge. My strength was that I could retain every assignment for each offensive position without losing focus on my own fullback duties. I was determined to memorize, visualize, and maximize that manual.

Some may think that I overdid it. But I wouldn't have it any other way. Over-preparing has always been my superpower. Whatever I lacked in raw talent, I made up for with tenacity. Your moment never arrives without putting in the hours to get there.

Growing up on the farm taught me plenty. When you feel like there is nothing left to do, no chore undone, there's always a fence or a tool that needs mending. Likewise, if you want to be a force on the football field, there is always one tool that is in constant need of adjustment—you.

Play Ball

After a solid three-hour nap, we had our first day of team meetings, walk thru, and practice. That schedule was followed by more position meetings and walk thru's. It was the fastest football that I have ever played.

There were no pads and supposedly no contact. We were out there to show speed, assignment execution, and effort. As a result of my studying, I had every play down and every snap count memorized. This allowed me to do what I did best—get off the ball and play fast. With the structure of play that the coaches set, I had no risk of injury to worry about.

My job as the fullback is to set the tempo and take the hit off my teammates. The first play I was in was a run play right up the heart of the defense. The play had the fullback heading straight for the middle linebacker. Since there was no real contact, most guys were backing down from hitting each other. Most were playing shifty to avoid contact rather than being aggressive. But as the fullback, I couldn't avoid contact, that was my job. I headed straight for the linebacker as fast as I could get off the ball. I didn't take him down or anything cheap, but I struck him. And from that point on, the coaches at least knew Zach Olstad was in Buffalo for rookie minicamp.

I was the only fullback at rookie camp with the Bills in 2018. And that was my biggest advantage. Being the only one at my position, I thought, if I could show my speed, power, and make the most of the opportunities in front of me, I might have a shot.

My official weight at minicamp was 248 pounds and I was running faster than I'd ever ran. Maybe it was the adrenaline, but as each opportunity came to me, I felt more confident. I literally had nothing to lose. This was my "one more" opportunity and I damn well knew it was likely my last one playing ball. That's when I heard a voice yelling for—"number 20!"

It hadn't been but 10 plays into rookie minicamp when I heard "20! 20!" Frantically I looked around, then I remembered I was wearing jersey 20. Having been #40 throughout the last six years of college, it didn't register at first. The voice yelling my number was the Head Coach, Sean McDermott.

I quickly ran up to Coach, and as I approached him I knew this could be a good moment, or a really bad one.

"Yes sir!" I ran towards him.

Looking down at his roster, he bellowed, " . . . and who are you?"

"Zach Olstad, sir."

"Where are you from?"

"I'm from Division II. Winona State University

in Winona, MN. My hometown is a small farm community called Harmony, also in Minnesota," I answered, not knowing if I was giving him much less or way more than necessary.

"What does your family do?"

I felt more confident with each question. "My Dad is a K-12 principal and a farmer, my Mom works at the same school as the district assessment coordinator, my brother and his wife also work at the same school as teachers, and my sister lives in Austin, TX and works in the food service industry," I said as quickly and clearly as I could. I wanted to make an impression; convey the diligence and efficiency of a motivated player. Looking him in the eye, I concluded, "I'm just a small-town kid who believes in God, Country, and Family."

With an affirmative nod, he offered, "I like that, now get back to work."

As I ran back to my running back coach, Coach Skipper asked, "What the hell was that all about?" I told him that Coach McDermott had a few questions for me, and I slipped back in the huddle.

The next play was my defining moment at rookie minicamp. Josh Allen was in at QB (seventh overall pick in 2018 draft) and we ran one of my favorite plays from the playbook.

As he called the play in the huddle, I knew this one could be coming to me. As Josh yelled "HUT" I took off with everything I had. My job was to run a wheel route up the sideline from the backfield. As I took off, I caught the eyes of the linebacker and knew I was in one-on-one coverage against him. The linebacker was within reach as I peeked over my left shoulder and saw the ball in the air.

It was headed my way. Josh hit me 25 yards down the sideline with a perfect, back shoulder throw. I leaped in the air, twisting to make the catch. When my feet hit the ground, I turned to protect the ball and I took off down the field as fast as I could.

When I came back to the huddle, I heard praise from both the coaches and players. Josh slapped me on the helmet. They could now see me as a fullback that could block, run, and catch.

After practice, I crossed paths with the offensive coordinator, Coach Brian Daboll, who added to my excitement. "Heck of a job today 20," he nodded. It was a short exchange, but it held weight. I felt a boost of confidence. I could compete with the big boys.

I was now comparable in strength and size, unlike my first couple seasons at Winona State. Still, I felt the need for more momentum. I needed to ramp it up even more. So, immediately after practice, I went to work on rehabbing my body to avoid injury.

After each practice, it was key to refuel your body with the proper nutrition and the Bills organization was first class when it came to taking care of their athletes. The facilities were unbelievable and unlike anything I had ever seen. At Winona State, there wasn't a budget for fancy amenities, sometimes at the small school we even battled with the general student population for space in the weight room. The Bills staff could tell that I was from a small school because every time there was something set out for us, I would politely ask permission to take one. There was food and drink everywhere, at all times. And if you needed anything at all, just ask.

I learned quickly that the players were treated like the engines and if the engines weren't fueled or taken care of properly, they wouldn't run like a champion. This privilege got my small-town personality laughed at a ton during my time in Buffalo because I'd never been treated like that before. Even so, my parents had raised me to say "please" and "thank you", and even at the highest level, being humble and polite go a long way.

Rookie minicamp goes quickly, especially when day one of three is travel and housekeeping. This was it, one last chance to make a lifetime of commitment to a goal come true, or it was time to go home. Being the only fullback was a huge advantage for me, but with increased reps comes increased risk for injuries.

Exclamation Point

At the beginning of our third day, Coach Skipper put the running backs through footwork drills. During the first drill, my knee started to act up for the first time during camp. I made one cut and felt it in my left knee. The pain caught me off guard and made me jump. I knew the injury from Arizona would catch up with me, I just didn't know when. What happened a few moments later almost sent me packing.

Behind the huddle, I would stay loose not knowing when my next opportunity to go in would be. I went to stretch my left knee which had the partial LCL and meniscus tear. Without thinking, I pulled my ankle to my butt to stretch my quad when I felt my knee slowly lock, I was stuck. I went quickly to the ground in pain, to try and unlock my knee which was glued in position.

The Bills trainers came over to me in a hurry. I cranked my leg into the position which, thankfully, unlocked my knee. But they were already on top of me asking what was going on. I stood up as quickly as I could, trying to act like nothing happened. If they thought that I was injured, I would've been dropped on my shield and sent home.

Both athletic trainers hit me with multiple questions. I told them I had a small cramp, in hopes they would leave me be. One trainer went to grab a cramp solution from their kit; a nasty liquid in a small plastic package. While the trainer went to grab the solution, the other pulled me aside and whispered to me, "Suck it the f*** up and get through today! They like you."

Luckily, I didn't miss any reps and was back in the huddle in no time. Moments like this brought me back to my first sports injury on my brother's Babe Ruth team. All I could hear was "Get Up," and keep moving forward.

I knew I needed one exclamation point before day three was over to give myself a chance. That opportunity came during one-on-ones against the defense.

I was lined up against a former Penn State linebacker. I ran a 3-way option route in which you judge the defender's body positioning and make a break at 5 yards, one of three ways. I put the linebacker on skates, gained separation from the defender, and Josh hit me as I took off up the field and outran the linebacker.

When I took off up the field, I ran right past Coach McDermott and Brandon Beane who was the General Manager. Each moment, whether it was a handshake, a play, or a pass, was an opportunity to make an impression.

After my conversation with our trainer, I knew that they were keeping an eye on me, and I was determined to finish strong.

The outcomes of those two practices were due to the habits I had been practicing all my life and career. A habit is something that is second nature, something that is innate to your being. You can't fake habits. My experience in the Amish house and life on the farm had taught me everything that I needed to know about an honest day's work. I carried that work ethic into my football career and over the years the ability to strain and give complete mental and physical effort, had become habitual to me.

I didn't have to summon this energy. With no pads, no refs, and limited contact, the one thing I did, every play, was show my home-grown instinct and run to the ball. No matter who caught it, I would sprint to them in a heartbeat, ready to block for them, lead them.

As I walked to the team huddle concluding our final practice, I wore a big grin underneath my helmet. I was just happy; no other words could describe the feeling of playing in the NFL, even if it was just for a couple days. Some people work their whole lives for that opportunity, and it never comes, but I got to live it.

After practice, Coach McDermott pulled both the squad and staff together for the final break-down. He thanked the tryout guys for coming, and offered, "Although the majority of you will not make the team, this will be a defining moment for you. Are you going to give up on your dreams? Or find another way to stay the course?"

Coach made it clear that if we were going to be signed to the team as a tryout player, a scout would approach us individually as we were leaving the field.

After the breakdown, I took it all in, as if that were the last time I would ever play football. Helmet in hand, I started walking off the field nice and slow. Out of the corner of my eye I saw someone beelining towards me and before I could turn, "Zach! You need to hustle to the locker room and meet Nate in the training room!"

I felt a whirlwind of hope and positive energy but wasn't completely sure what was going on. I could be getting signed, they could be doing a test on my body and injuries, or maybe someone wanted to just say their goodbyes. I had no idea.

The tryout players were in a separate locker room away from the practice facilities, so I had quite the run before I could get back to the training room. I can still feel my heart racing as my cleats galloped across the facilities parking lot to grab my stuff. I took a minute shower, from head to toe. I started shaking, no one else was around.

I didn't know what was about to happen. But I felt like I was living the best part of a movie.

As I sat down, I could feel how heavy my legs were and the throbbing trauma in my knee. That's when Nate, the head trainer, walked in, smiling. The office we were in was separated from the others by a glass wall. And when I looked around, all the other trainers were looking in at us, as if we were the afternoon's entertainment.

I couldn't wait any longer. Turning to Nate I exhaled, "What's going on man?"

Glancing at the guys on the other side of the glass, Nate turned to me and winked, "Zach, you're in the NFL."

It was a moment, an achievement that had seemed unthinkable for so long. I had proved that it wasn't impossible.

Every trainer congratulated me, and Nate finished off with a little added news; "Out of the thirty tryout rookies attending this minicamp, you are the only one being signed to the Buffalo Bills."

***

#OlstadsInsteads

A person's true colors will eventually show. Instead of being someone you are not, always be true to you.

That's when I heard a voice yelling for, "number 20!" Having been #40 throughout the past 6 years of college it didn't register at first. Looking down at his roster, the coach bellowed, "Who are you?" Looking him in the eye, "I'm just a small-town kid who believes in God, Country, and Family."

9

Organized Team Activities

This was more than football. This was an opportunity of a lifetime. But before the thrill of 'The Contract', there was the inevitable drill of 'The Physical.'

With my long history of injuries, I had to sign two waivers: for my left shoulder and foot. The x-rays clearly showed that my left foot was held together by a well-placed screw. But after explaining that I had played my collegiate senior season on it, the doctors let me off the hook. All I had to do was sign an agreement that if I re-injure my prior injuries, it was not on the team's dime to fix them.

Whew! With that out of the way, it was now time for my NFL contract, or so I thought.

The Bills planned to offer me to a 3-year rookie deal with a signing bonus. The only hold up was that they would not be able to sign me just yet. The staff explained that they had a full roster. The Bills would first have to cut a player for me to replace, and that process could take a day or two.

Until the team made their decision, I was only to inform my immediate family. So, I shot a quick text to my Mom that I would "not be coming home for a while." Later that night I finally got to talk with my family, virtually. My parents spoke of spending the last day of rookie minicamp driving around Winona, parking at Maxwell Field in view of the Warrior Shield; sitting, praying, and believing it would be "my time."

When I let them know that their prayers had been answered, it was a moment none of us will ever forget. It was the fulfillment of a journey that had taken us all to unimaginable places.

***

Two days later it was announced to the public that the Buffalo Bills had signed Rookie Fullback, Zach Olstad. When the news broke, we were in the middle of the morning walk-thru and lift. Once I got back to the locker room, my phone was going off. I was proud and wanted to take a moment to celebrate, but I had a job to do. I was in the midst of the highest high of my life, while trying to stay calm and collected at work. There was no time to let it sink in.

Immediately following rookie minicamp, Organized Team Activities (OTAs) were already rolling, and we had a full month of work ahead of us. I would be in the running back room with former pro bowl talent LeSean McCoy, Patrick DiMarco, and Chris Ivory along with other veteran NFL running backs including Taiwan Jones, Marcus Murphey, Travaris Cadet, and rookie Keith Ford.

Before being signed I was aware that in front of me would be veteran fullback, Patrick DiMarco. A staple in the NFL, a guy I could learn from. In the end, there would only be one of us left standing as NFL teams normally don't carry two fullbacks. Pat was the type of teammate who helped me every time it was needed and was always sharing valuable advice for a young fullback. He was first class.

At the time, I was thinking this is the hardest physical and mental workout I had ever experienced. The day's schedule was full: practice, meetings, lifts, training room, more meetings. And at night I had hours of studying to do on the complex playbook —all while trying to keep my weight up. Once I understood my responsibilities and was able to organize my time efficiently, I was able to enjoy both the workouts and timeouts with my new teammates.

With weekends off, it allowed us to explore Buffalo. To me, the city was huge, but it also had that "Minnesota nice" feel to it. One of my favorite memories in Buffalo, outside of football, was going to a country concert with teammates. It was a dream for a small-town kid like me. Up in a private suite with my teammates enjoying country music.

Everyone caught on that I was a simple, small-town kid. Maybe it was because I knew I was an underdog, and to stay on the squad I needed to keep my mouth shut and bust my ass. I think that they appreciated my authenticity.

During OTAs there were two busses for the rookies to take home at night. One bus left immediately after the day was done, the other left later in the afternoon. I always stuck around for the late bus.

One night, during the first week of OTAs, I ran into Coach McDermott. There was nobody else around, just the Coach and me. The conversation between us was brief but memorable, with more than a few laughs. "Isn't this great," he grinned. "We woke up with jobs in the NFL, who's got it better than us?!" That brief exchange left me with so much respect for Coach McDermott. He was blue collar, respectful; a guy who genuinely cared about his players. I knew that he knew, I was a long shot. But he gave me an even opportunity to compete.

Absolute Animals with Intention

How you carried yourself in the facility said more about your character than anything else. To help us newcomers on our journey, we engaged in rookie player development meetings after practice. As part of this, speakers came in to inspire us. Former players and other professionals would give us advice on "how to be an NFL player" and what to expect, post-career. It was fun getting to know both the guys, their backgrounds, and how to maximize our time on and off the NFL field.

Of all the rookie development meetings, my favorite was done by an organization called 'Galvanize.' Laura Okmin, a veteran NFL broadcasting commentator, brought in aspiring women reporters, who were each paired with one of us rookie players. After a brief introduction with our reporter, we were interviewed about our journey in front of the team. This was lights, camera, action, and all eyes were on you. Hearing the different backgrounds, stories, and journeys that my teammates had experienced, helped me to respect each individual, on a personal level.

With the busy schedule, we didn't always get to look around and appreciate each other, because we were always on the move. Our time with the

Galvanize Organization helped us slow down and get to know each other, which built brotherhood within the rookie class.

Although the end goal was to individually make the team, coaches and veteran players made it clear that rookies needed to help each other out as well. Within our ranks, we used the brother system to help us recognize, reset, and refocus. Every rookie was going to be challenged and experience adversity. It was just a matter of time.

There were constant "welcome to the NFL" moments.

My first was in the weight room. I vividly remember standing next to Kelvin Benjamin before starting our lift and thinking to myself, "How the hell am I in the NFL?" I was a fullback at 5'11" and 245 pounds and Kelvin was literally 6'5" and similar in weight to a wide receiver. Another vivid "welcome" was seeing a lineman bench over 400 pounds for several reps.

The atmosphere in an NFL weight room is different from anything I had experienced in my career. I was surrounded by absolute animals with intentional focus. It didn't matter if it was pre-practice or post-practice, we got after it. Everything mattered. You were held to the highest standard at all times. And the most important of all was, The Playbook.

I had heard that NFL playbooks were much more in-depth and complicated than college playbooks—that was an understatement. They installed new plays every single day, with new flavors to already installed plays, along with new snap counts and responsibilities. It can be complicated and confusing. Overall, I understood the playbook well. Still, I took hours, every night, to perfect the upcoming day's install.

Close Call

I was ready. Even my long list of injuries through college prepared me for the next level. I would spend hours at night rehabbing my body with trainers to ensure proper recovery. OTAs "no contact" rule gave my body time to catch up on some of these nagging injuries. But unfortunately, all it took was one unexpected hit.

During our no-pads practice, I split out wide and ran a five-yard "hook" route. At the top of my route, I saw the ball in the air and went up to snag it. In mid-air I was hit from behind and proceeded to land on my left knee. In a hurry, I tried to stand up as all eyes were on me, but something in my knee was not right. Once again, my knee was intensely locked.

Within a split second of standing, I knew what I needed to do. I flashbacked to my CFL tryout and remembered how I reset my knee into proper position. In front of the team and everyone at practice, ball still in one hand, I pulled up my leg and rotated my knee with my other hand and felt an instantaneous release. When my leg returned to its correct position, I ran back to the huddle, ready for more.

But ... not so fast.

Two trainers, including the head trainer, immediately told me that I was out. They took me to the side as I repeated "I'm fine, just landed on my knee wrong." One of the trainers, with doubt in his eye, motioned for me to "prove it."

I ran through a series of sprints, cuts, and jumps to assure them that it was nothing serious. Deep down, I knew that something was definitely wrong, and that I had been lucky each time it allowed me to re-position. This was my risk, and my dream. And as Dad always said, "It's a long way from your heart."

The trainers gave me the go ahead to rejoin the team and re-enter play. Fellow coaches, players, and staff asked if I was alright. I assured them that I had just caught my knee wrong.

Post-practice I was walking alongside Pat DiMarco and he advised me, "Make sure the coaches know you're fine. Prove it to them. Otherwise, they may go shopping for a replacement."

Sure enough, the coaches and trainers requested that I join them in the training room. As they ran their tests on my knee, I looked at them square in the eye, "I'm fine." I got out of there without my knee re-catching. But I still had two days left of OTAs to prove my knee was healthy.

It had been the most exhausting month—and yet the best month of my life. But the mental and physical intensity of OTAs would not compare to what was coming . . . Training Camp.

***

#OlstadsInsteads

Don't let your guard down. Instead, understand you are always being evaluated.

How you carry yourself says more about your character than the clothes you wear.

10

Driven

Why did I refuse to quit? What was left for me to prove? What's the real reason I put my body, my soul, through the trauma? Who was it for? Was it all worth it? Going home for a month gave me the chance to refocus. It helped me to re-evaluate my "why."

***

Before leaving Buffalo, I was given an accountability contract that listed my strengths and areas that needed improvement. At the top of my "strength list" was my work ethic. Not talent, but the rudiments of my upbringing. With that in mind, I took a deep breath and once again found the rhythm in the grind.

During that month home, three times a week I would get up at 3am and drive from Harmony, MN to Oakdale, MN to train with Trevor Glomski, at ETS. But I wasn't the only one getting up at 3am. After I took a shower and made sure my bags were packed, I'd walk downstairs to find Mom with a smile on her face and breakfast on the table. With a two-and-a-half-hour road trip ahead, my morning cook would always serve up a huge meal: four to six scrambled eggs, sausage or ham, fruit, yogurt and grains, oatmeal, banana, an avocado, and a protein shake.

Mom knew what she was doing.

Leaving OTAs, every player had to sign a contract that included their "fine weight." Coming into training camp my weight had to be between 240–245 pounds, and for every pound I was over I would be fined $700. It was the intent of Buffalo's Strength and Nutrition Staff that my weight and body stay finely tuned. I could not afford the $700 per pound fine, so you can bet I was weighing myself daily, till I had it down to a science. Years of effort, both on the farm and field, had molded me into being specific when it came to maintaining my goals and accountability.

Vehicle of My Vision

The days I drove, I had plenty of time to think. The commute enabled me to recognize, reset and refocus. The road gave me the space to mentally prepare, to work through the vision board in my head. Driving between training sessions was cathartic. The practice started back when I would commute to Winona during college.

I knew nothing was going to be handed to me growing up on the farm, nobody else was going to stack my bales. It was up to me to take the wheel. On those drives, I literally chased my dreams.

In between those commutes, there was no slowing down. There was a stack of study materials next to my bed. Often, I would fall asleep in the same studious position, running through each play, over and over. Training camp was around the corner, and I could not afford to miss any assignments. This was not going to be a no-pads OTA. This was war.

One of the most difficult areas of the playbook was over one hundred "speed plays." These plays were meant for time-sensitive situations, such as the "two-minute drill," or whenever we needed a quick score. The majority of these plays were triggered by a one-word command, or a silent signal. When the quarterback yelled the word, or the signal flashed from the sidelines, we were to execute the correct formation, alignment, and know the assignment instantly, without huddling. Without repetition and dedication, these plays could be a player's worst nightmare. The NFL playbook was a juggernaut.

When I first saw The Playbook, I was blown away by its intricacies and volume. Growing up in a small town, almost everyone with a shred of athletic ability played all three seasons of sports. To simplify things, the local school playbooks were short and simple—if there was one at all. I first learned the in-depth X's and O's of the game during college. In the NFL, the plays and patterns were, to put it simply, more complicated.

To hold myself accountable, I was in contact with my position Coach, Coach Skipper, and teammate, Pat DiMarco, weekly throughout the month at home. Driven to make sure my focus was consistent, and that we were all on the same page, those calls were intense.

I didn't know what to expect at training camp, because I'd never physically been through one.

But for sure it was going to be a brutal competition. Whoever was chosen for the regular season roster would be putting food on the table for their family. We were a team, but every man had to fight for his place.

Home Teams

In the blink of an eye, I had only two weeks left at home. And Summer was the farm's busy season. During this time, we would vaccinate the livestock, preg-check the cattle, and spend those hot days doing the countless little jobs necessary to ready both the farm, and the land, for another Minnesota winter.

Throughout the month, Dad and Levi were extra careful not to let me do anything that would put me at risk of an injury. It felt unusual to move around our farm with such caution. Typically, I would be in the pen with the cattle, pushing them through the corral. But cattle can be unpredictable, and I would need both hands to count how many times a cow has kicked at me.

So, I stayed on the sidelines and watched my family do the dirty work.

***

As a kid, I would attend Minnesota Vikings Training Camp to catch a glimpse of NFL players like Randy Moss, Chris Carter, and Adrian Peterson. Watching them at Training Camp I often imagined, if I tried really hard, that I could be in their shoes someday. The dream took a while, but that day eventually showed up, just before I left for training camp.

As I was making my final preparations to leave

Harmony for Rochester, NY, the head coach of my high school team, invited me to their youth football camp. Coach Mensink asked that I come and have a chat with the current crop of up and comers of the Fillmore Central Falcons.

Looking out at the young faces trying to get a glimpse of me, I did my best to cram a lifetime of lessons into a few minutes. I advised the kids to be coachable, in football and in all aspects of life. I stressed the importance of showing respect for their teachers, custodians, and coaches. Heeding advice is important. The moment you think you know it all—THAT's when you stop growing.

The eyes of forty young kids were on me as I explained that there is no 'team' without camaraderie. To be a great player, you must first be a good individual and a good teammate. Support each other. Celebrate one another's successes, and be there to lift each other up, because we all fall. Athletics don't make you—You do. Find purpose beyond the game, in something bigger than football —something larger than yourself.

"Stay the course." Knowing the struggles, they would soon face, I cautioned them not to stray from their dreams. Learn from others, but don't try to be someone else. Whatever drives you, put your shoulder into it, push until your determination transforms you into the best version of YOU.

At the end of the day, working hard got me further than talent. Clearly it took some ability, but I found a work ethic that my body could handle, and I ran with it. It was grueling, tiring, and some-times painful. But your body will respond. It can adapt to the difficult. Nothing in my life's success has come from warm, comfortable situations.

I told them of the Warrior Code and of the vision I set for myself: Whatever you attempt, give it everything you got.

***

A few days later, as I carried my bags into the airport, I realized I was literally on my way to do battle. In my pocket was the ticket to my destination, the culmination of a dream that had driven me to this moment, to this flight.

I was on my way to fight for my position, and I was prepared to practice what I preached.

***

#OlstadsInsteads

Instead of cutting corners, take a risk and go the distance.

"Whatever drives you, put your shoulder into it, push until your determination transforms you into the best version of YOU."

11

Stumble Forward

There is an old adage that says, *"A step is a stumble forward, which is prevented from becoming a fall by taking another step."*

***

NFL Training Camp would be the most trying experience of my life. The steepest of mountains. The hardest climb. The only thing that kept me from stumbling, was my foundation and decades of stored up determination. Though tired, I kept putting one foot in front of the other. The alternative was unthinkable.

St. John Fischer College in Rochester, New York was the site for the Buffalo Bills training camp. This would be my home for the next month before we headed back to Buffalo to finish the pre-season. Training camp is about building camaraderie, competition, and finalizing the roster. The first person that I saw upon arrival was the head coach, Sean McDermott. He shook my hand and said, "Hope you're ready to roll." That exchange solidified my "1/11th" promise to the Bills organization, that I will do anything to help the team. But before you can help a team, you have to prove that you are ready to be a part of it.

To kick off training camp was the conditioning test. The test was timed 100-yard sprints (50 yards and back). Each position had a different time criteria to meet. Failure to reach these simple expectations resulted in daily conditioning following practice until you prove that you're in top shape. In a sense, this was an accountability test. To prove that I was ready, I sprinted, sticking with the front of the pack. I would stay after practice to condition, work on technique and run routes with the quarterbacks when time allowed. That extra effort on the field is noticed by the coaches. Those who strive for greatness at any profession arrive early and stay late. On the farm, I learned that you don't quit until the job is done, and it's never easy to meet those demands. To plant your flag on the summit of your journey will take everything you've got and then some.

Nothing that I've experienced held a nickel next to training camp. Not the longest day on the hay wagon stacking bales with my family. Not even playing through four games with a broken foot. Although these grueling experiences shaped my mindset, I knew I could stumble through anything, if I remained determined to take another step.

New players arrived daily to take the position of hurt or released players. There was a constant cycle of meetings, walk-thru's, practices, meals, lifts, and drug tests. Followed by more meetings, and more practice. On Wednesday nights, players would have the option to attend Team Prayer with Team Chaplain, Len Vanden Bos. This was a time to recognize, reset, and refocus through the grind.

To sit back and count our blessings so that while we hustle, we remain humble.

Just like OTAs in June, there was a structured agenda. Most mornings I would get up at 5:30am or earlier, and train well into the night. I would conclude the day studying in my dorm, spending hours running through my assignments, never knowing when there might be a knock at the door, with the worst kind of news for a football player.

Discipline was the key to training camp. It was a daily competition, mostly with yourself. This pressure can eat at your ability to adapt, recover, and continue. With the daily stress, lack of sleep, and the physical demands, it was hard to keep my weight up. Before lifts and practices, players weighed themselves as part of the nutrition/strength plan. If your weight is dropping too much, you will be put into a calorie surplus to get back to your proper weight range. My range was 240-245 pounds. This goal was far-fetched, especially after an intense practice with full pads in the heat. Some days I would return to the locker room 8 pounds lighter. I was constantly gorging to stay afloat.

As players' bodies began to wear down, the mental side of the game revs up. When men are in a fight for their jobs, the competition becomes tangible. You can feel it in the air. In that tense atmosphere, you are bound to get run over. But never dwell on one bad play, focus on consistency.

An error only becomes a mistake if you fail to fix it. There were times during training camp when I got beat, and the coaches got on my ass. Take the criticism. Learn from it. Improve quickly. Be coachable. Move forward.

The real problem is when nobody is hounding you to improve. That's when you should start to worry.

Poor Side of the Pool

Rookies are constantly reminded that they're small fish in a very big pond. The new guys are usually given the privilege of carrying the veterans' gear off the field after practices. And a lucky few are chosen to keep the meeting rooms stocked with snacks. Within the first week of training camp, this rare honor was delegated to me. The only problem was that nobody gave me money for the mission and my bank account was next to nothing.

With no vehicle at camp, I had to borrow one of the veteran's cars. It was so fancy I didn't even know how to start it! Eventually, I figured out that the "key" to the 21st century rocket ship was a button. And if that discovery wasn't illuminating enough, the sight of the monitor rising out of the dashboard, proved to me that I was a long way from home. "Hmmm," I chuckled, "You don't see that in Amish Country."

As I returned to camp from my grocery run, I was in a hurry to beat the curfew—and its accompanying fine. Let's just say it was a constant work out to make my "privilege" a noticeable splash in the pond.

We were all teammates, but also competitors for the same goal. We all knew that the Bills rookie pool would not hold us all. Every day of Training Camp was our one chance to make a big splash. And our biggest opportunity to do that, was the scrimmage at the Bills Stadium, right before the start of pre-season play.

Keith Ford, our rookie running back, was lined up behind me as we ran the ball into the defense. As Keith made his cut and took it the distance, I chased him as fast as I could to secure the hustle award. For what felt like an 80-yard sprint, I ran faster, harder than I ever had in memory. Exhausted, I finally found him in the endzone.

As we were jogging to the sideline for a much-needed breather, I heard my name called for the next play. I had to go back in. My heart was thumping through my shoulder pads. It was one of my longest runs ever. I was desperate for air. I was done, spent, completely out of breath for that next play. But, somehow, I made it to the huddle at the other end of the field and did my job.

As I came off the field, Pat DiMarco (starting fullback) and Coach Skipper (running backs coach) were looking in my direction laughing. "You need to chill out bro." They knew I just ran the distance with Keith. Though in serious need of oxygen, I did my best to laugh with them. I had no idea I was going right back into the game.

That hustle got me noticed. It was my little splash in the pond; the kind of extra effort that can get you noticed.

Game Day

Our first pre-season matchup, with the Carolina Panthers, was finally here. My family was finally coming to town. I was about to live out my child-hood dream.

The night before, we had a meeting in the hotel where Coach McDermott spoke on our team character, expectations, and what the plan was for game day. My nerves came and went as I watched film and took one last look over my responsibilities.

When the wakeup call came the following morning, I felt like a kid on Christmas. It was game day, and I was in the NFL about to play with the big boys, in front of thousands.

Dressed to impress in my clearance JC Penney slacks and collared shirt, I climbed aboard the team bus, which was escorted from the hotel to the stadium by a parade of flashing blue and red lights, like we were royalty. About this same time my family was being seated in the stands. They couldn't believe how well they were treated in Buffalo. Their every need was anticipated. My folks had access to the player's family parking lot, special seats in the stadium, passes for post-practice and game meals, and someone was always near to help them in any way. When it comes to taking care of a player's family, The Bills Organization was first class.

Before walking out on the field, a rush of emotion came over me. This was the day I had dreamed about in the barn, bailing hay, in that old weight room, pulling cinderblocks, and on the front porch, pacing. And now my parents were in the stadium, waiting. It was the best feeling in the world.

Jogging out into the massive stadium for warm-ups, I was met by a wall of screaming fans that earned the name, "Bills Mafia." Everything was a blur till my eye caught a glimpse of my family. It felt like an eternity since I had last seen them. My brother, Levi, was the first face I recognized, and up on his shoulders was my four-year-old niece, Madeline, screaming "Zachary! Zachary!" I laughed inside and displayed a big smile, immersed in the overwhelming reality of it all.

The moment of revelry soon passed. And joining my teammates, I took my earned position on the field. The Coach had informed me that the second, third and fourth quarters were mine as fullback. Having spent a lifetime preparing, I was more than ready. And so was our competition, the Carolina Panthers.

***

During that first quarter, on the sidelines, I flashed back to an early lesson as a walk-on at Winona State. "To be a leader on the field, first be a leader on the bench." Thinking of this, my attention was riveted to the guys on the gridiron, watching every move of the fullback in front of me, and being a helpful teammate when they came off the field. Likewise, every time Pat stepped off the field, he gave me tangible advice for my turn in the game. Then, though it seemed only seconds had passed, the first quarter whistle blew. We had the lead . . .

My time had arrived. For the rest of the game, I was Buffalo's work horse.

Putting on my helmet, I headed for the quarter-back who was forming the huddle. As he emphasized the play call, my job was simple, and I had plenty adrenaline to wear off. The game was flying by.

In a blink of an eye, it was Halftime, and we were off to the locker room to rehydrate, grab a snack, and make adjustments for the second half. Normally, these tweaks were related to the play-book and how the opposing team was lining up against us. But I had another issue: my bad foot, the one I broke in college. As I listened to the coaches, I could feel my tape job digging into my screw, protruding into the edge of my cleat. With help of the trainers, we pulled off my taped-on cleat on my already beat up and previously surgically fixed foot to find my socks covered in blood. During the first half, I could feel the tape ripping up my skin. The area that I had my foot surgery protrudes further out than the rest of my foot. We covered my broken skin from the constant rubbing and tearing with gauze, re-taped, and I was ready to roll for the second half of play. An uncomfortable feeling, but with my adrenaline pumping, the only thing I hoped for was that the second half of the game would slow down. Not because I was in pain, but because this was my first game in the NFL. I didn't want it to be over.

Back on the gridiron, I was in and out of the game throughout the entire second half. Anxiously I hovered around the bench; watching, waiting, anticipating our offensive coaches' signal to get back onto the field. For those three hours of work, I was fully attentive. I couldn't help but celebrate every teammate's success. After constantly battling with teammates, fighting for our jobs during training camp, we were now one team, battling the Panthers.

Over the years, I learned that sacrificing for your teammates, supporting them, helps both the giver and receiver. When you only see one person in the mirror, nothing changes. But when you eventually realize you are not the only one on the field, that's when things start to move. Being selfless ignites an internal drive. And it always pushes you in the right direction, for all the right reasons.

The duties of a fullback often go unnoticed. We lead the way for the running backs and clean up the line of scrimmage to give the quarterback the time, the elbow room, to make the play. For me to reach this position required minimal talent. I was here solely due to stubborn grit, consistency, and the determined inability to quit. Although, the position was nothing glamorous, it was "me" in a nutshell. Every chance I got on that field I gave it every ounce of effort I had.

As I walked off of the field following my first NFL game, I took in the moment, nice and slow, putting one foot in front of the other. It was reminiscent of my last day at rookie minicamp, when I walked off thinking it was over. Then, out of the blue, that scout stopped me with an invitation to a locker room full of blue.

***

A couple days later we were back to work preparing for the Cleveland Browns. My body was sore, but nothing I hadn't been through before. I continued to push my old injuries to their limits, always keeping in mind the nagging notion of the inevitable.

I always imagined it would be the foot screw breaking, my shoulder giving out, or my battered knee finally failing. But all those tangled rigs of paper clips and chewing gum stayed intact. What I didn't expect was an ordinary drill, not the sort you find on a work bench in the family barn, but the kind you face on a practice field going head-to-head with a herd of buffalo.

During that drill, versus the defense, I climbed to the safety during a run play, and as my cleats planted to block the defender, my foot stuck oddly in the ground. Similar to how my left foot broke in college, my right ankle took a turn for the worst. As my heel rotated inward, I dropped to the ground in excruciating pain. The audible "pop" reverberated through my leg like an electrocution.

As I hobbled to the bench, the coach pointed back to the field, "You good to go?" It seemed to take me forever to answer. I knew something was wrong, but how bad? Pat leaned in, "I'll take this one." And with a slap of concern on my shoulder, he ran onto the field to join the huddle.

The pain, I could handle. But the function of my ankle was like a newborn calf, weak and unstable. The training staff attempted to put me through a few drills, but I was eventually escorted to the team doctor's tent.

The tests clearly showed a sprain and ligament instability. But was it broke? Within the hour, I was transported from training camp back to Buffalo for imaging. After the MRI and x-rays, it was clear: a high ankle sprain.

I tried to tell myself, " . . . if I could play out the remainder of a season in college with a broken foot, I can handle a sprained ankle." But deep down I knew this was not my call. It was the Bills decision. And I was sidelined, in a walking boot.

The following day was quiet. I spent most of it in the weight room with the strength staff. I could feel it in the air, a sense of separation. Talking with Nate, the man who informed me I was being signed after rookie minicamp, I straight up asked him, "Am I going to get cut?"

"Zach, it doesn't look good. In my experience, they're already shopping."

As I juggled calls with my agents and family, I was, of course, disappointed, but tried to stay calm. I knew the final whistle was coming, but when? This wound would take a long time to heal and so would the ankle.

The following morning, at team breakfast, I could barely stir my coffee for all of the players and coaches offering me their hand and support. "I respect your play," the offensive coordinator, Brian Daboll added, "You work your ass off."

When I was finally about to raise my not-so-steaming cup, a man approached and politely asked if I could follow him to meet with Coach. To most, it would have seemed a walk of shame. But I stood tall, shifted my weight off my injured foot and followed.

As the two of us started down the hall, we passed team chaplain, Len Vanden Bos, who, sensing the solemn atmosphere, wrinkled his brow with concern. "Hey! Zach, what's going on?" Without breaking the rhythm of my hobble, I gestured ahead, "Not sure, but I think I'm being released." Understanding the moment, the Chaplain dropped what he was doing, turned, fell in behind us, and matched my every stumble-step to the Coach's door.

Inside the office sat Coach McDermott, with the Bills General Manager, Brandon Beane. As we shook hands, we all knew what was coming.

"Zach, you know what we have to do here," Beane broke the ice.

"Yes sir," I struggled to smile, feeling both grateful and empty.

"You're being released due to the seriousness of your ankle injury. The settlement will be handled with your agents. Think of it like workman's comp."

"The last thing I'm concerned about is money. I understand and want you both to know that giving me this opportunity changed my life for the better. I will forever be in your debt."

As we stood up, I held out my hand. Instead, Coach McDermott pulled me in for a hug.

Outside the office door, the world seemed too big to pick a direction. After a moment to get my bearings, I realized that Chaplain Len was still there, waiting. And with a tone of respect that was, frankly, unexpected, he asked, "Walk you out?"

The man escorted me like I was royalty.

From an Amish farm, surrounded by crops, to a field of grass measured off with chalk, I had traveled a roller-coaster rabbit trail of pain and progress. And having endured the lessons of both, I glimpsed what few dare to see; the true measure of my worth. And if anyone understood what that mix of knowledge can do to someone—for someone, both without and within, it was my escort, Chaplain Len, the man walking next to the guy limping. For in those few amazing moments that we were side-by-side, he could see that my every stride was a stumble forward, a journey that had always been prevented from becoming a fall by simply having the faith to take another step.

*** **** ***

As the Chaplain and I walked, I realized my journey was proof that no matter the dream, nothing was impossible. And that, like a work horse in the field, I would soon be back on the farm, back on the front porch, pacing, planning, ready, and ever willing to take another step . . . forward.

#OlstadsInsteads

Why stay at home with a pillow full of dreams, when you can come back home with a duffel bag of memories, *instead.*

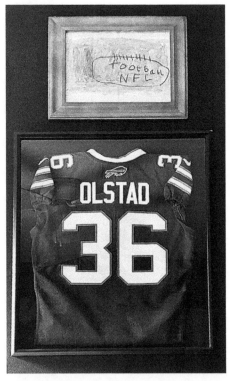

"Looking at that 20-year-old drawing and the many strides I've made since then, I realized that my childhood dream had been unthinkable, unbelievable, and well worth the fight."

Epilogue

I had survived my quest and fulfilled my dream. I got to play with the big boys. I had been there, done that, and not only bought the t-shirt, but earned the number on my blue, Buffalo Bills uniform. Now, having climbed my mountain and planted my flag, I only needed to pick the best direction to put this wealth of knowledge and experience to work. And before me was an unexplored world of options.

The aches and pains from my previous career are a constant reminder of my true purpose. I sacrificed and learned the hard way so that I can serve others on their journey.

Following my football journey, I moved to Nashville, Tennessee where I have started a mobile fitness company, 4x4 Fitness. To grow this business will take the same foundation that my football journey took and then some. Football instilled a sense of urgency in me that I can't turn off. Whether it's my business, books, or side hustles, I am always on the move. I have plans to travel the country and speak at schools, communities, and organizations where I can inspire and continue to make an impact as I serve others. The role that I have created gives me the opportunity to be a fullback, daily. A fullback of life where I can lead and give ultimate effort to others and help them create a path to personal success. No matter the profession, I have always had the same end goal in mind.

I want a life where I found out who I was. A life deep in the country, where we spend the summers balin' and if you blink while driving through you'll miss it. Where tourists find the landscape boring, but our work is never done. Where one day I can let my children drive in a field at age six, the same way I did. A place to teach my kids how to work with nothing fancy. The same place I became a Work Horse.

***

Acknowledgements

To my Dad, Mom, Brother, Sister, Julia, Madeline and Samuel . . . You've seen the struggle, you've stuck with me to the mountain top, and witnessed me fall back to the bottom, just to get back up and try again. No matter what, you've always been by my side and believed when so many people didn't. Without you, this story wouldn't have come to life. I love you more. Thank You.

To Melody, for all the help with this project. Taking it from the rough draft it was, to a piece of art that was editable. You are truly the most genuine person I've met and asked nothing in return. Although, you couldn't make many of the games, I feel this was your moment in the stands, and to me, that is just as important. Thank you for all the help as this project took shape.

Barton Green . . . even though you hate the word, you are "awesome." The editor of *Work Horse* and a lifelong friend of mine. For the knowledge, wisdom, and 3am calls, I will always be thankful. You made this story come to life and truly made it a masterpiece. Thank you.

Kristina Russo and Laura Okmin...for encouraging me to tell my story. You believed this story could inspire others and that inspired me to put pen to paper. Thank you.

Len, Coach McDermott, Coach Sawyer, Coach Keller, Brandon Beane...

Entire Bills Organization...

Winona State Football Teammates, Coaches and Staff...

Fillmore Central Schools...

Grandparents...

Harmony, Minnesota...

Keith Johnson...

Howard Wells...

Jennie Hefren...

Zach Olstad is an author, business owner, and former professional athlete. Olstad has a degree in K-12 Education, is a certified personal trainer, motivational speaker, and farmer.

Originally from the small town of Harmony, Minnesota, Olstad currently lives in Nashville, Tennessee where he operates his fitness company, 4x4 Fitness.

Olstad learned how to reach his goals with minimal resources, trusting and relying on his obsessive work ethic to see him through. He was molded by an internal drive at a young age that has carried him to unimaginable places.

Share a picture of yourself with the book,
Work Horse.

Instagram @zach_olstad

TikTok @zach_olstad

Twitter @zach_olstad

www.zacholstad.com

***